The POWER to HEAL

ANGELA COOPER

BALBOA.
PRESS
A DIVISION OF HAY HOUSE

Scripture quotations are taken from the Holy Bible, New Living Translation, copyright
©1996, 2004, 2007, 2013, 2015 by Tyndale House Foundation. Used by permission of
Tyndale House Publishers, Inc., Carol Stream, Illinois 60188. All rights reserved.

Balboa Press books may be ordered through booksellers or by contacting:

Balboa Press
A Division of Hay House
1663 Liberty Drive
Bloomington, IN 47403
www.balboapress.com
1 (877) 407-4847

Because of the dynamic nature of the Internet, any web addresses or
links contained in this book may have changed since publication and
may no longer be valid. The views expressed in this work are solely those
of the author and do not necessarily reflect the views of the publisher,
and the publisher hereby disclaims any responsibility for them.

The author of this book does not dispense medical advice or prescribe the use
of any technique as a form of treatment for physical, emotional, or medical
problems without the advice of a physician, either directly or indirectly. The
intent of the author is only to offer information of a general nature to help you
in your quest for emotional and spiritual well-being. In the event you use any
of the information in this book for yourself, which is your constitutional right,
the author and the publisher assume no responsibility for your actions.

Any people depicted in stock imagery provided by Thinkstock are models,
and such images are being used for illustrative purposes only.
Certain stock imagery © Thinkstock.

Print information available on the last page.

ISBN: 978-1-5043-6078-4 (sc)
ISBN: 978-1-5043-6079-1 (e)

Balboa Press rev. date: 10/27/2016

Contents

Dedication

To all great generals of the gospel who have labored before us, may this book reflect the countless hours in you have spent seeking the face of our King for this generation.

To my great grandmother, the late Annie-Mae Jones alias 'Ma Ma' - may my life reflect the legacy and memories of the life that you lived, as a woman who greatly feared and reverenced her God. You truly lived a kingdom-life marked with prayer and consecration. I know that your time with the King has changed everything, and you are now enjoying royalty at its best.

To my grandmother, the late Sophie Ervin alias 'Ma Ma' Sophie - your life continues to be an inspiration to me. I am so blessed to have had you in my life. As I reflect, I am reminded of the many fishing trips you took me on as a child. I valued the time spent, sitting patiently waiting by the bank for the fish to bite. I did not realize it then, but I know now that it was one of my many preparations for serving the King!

> "For they that wait upon the Lord, He shall renew their strength, they shall mount up with wings as an eagle, they shall run and not be weary and they shall walk and not faint." Isaiah 40:31

I am so grateful for the opportunity to share the last moments with you, before beginning your new life with the King.

To my late grandmother Ms. Catherine Pruitt alias 'Grandma Cat'- your life holds the greatest story on this side of heaven; of the faithfulness, and greatness of our God. I can hear you saying, *"I thank God for all my children, and my grandchildren too. I pray all my children live a long healthy life."*

I will never forget the day you called; the voice I heard was filled with glorious joy saying *"Angie I'm healed. I can walk. Jesus has healed me, and I knew he could do it."* I honor and praise God for your never-ending faith and confidence in Him. Thank you for always praying for me. For this, and so much more, I honor you. I miss you dearly.

To my Great King, the Lord Jesus Christ. I am mesmerized by your love. The very thought of you loving me overwhelms me at times. You captivate my heart. There is nobody like, or greater than You, who takes my breath away. May Your kingdom come, and Your will be done in earth, (me) as it is in heaven.

Acknowledgement

This book was birth through my experience with God's healing power, and witnessing that same miraculous power heal many. I can truly say as David, "Many are the afflictions of the righteous, but God delivers him out of them all" **Psalms 34:19**.

To my children, Javaris, Abigail and Jeremiah, you three are the greatest children on earth. God saw fit to bless me with the utmost honor of birthing the three of you. My earnest prayer is that I build a dynasty, leaving you a legacy that will influence your generation and beyond. My desire is that you continue to pursue God with all your heart, mind, soul and body. You belong to Him. Stay focused on Him and you will reach the maximum potential you have envisioned. I absolutely love you, just because I do.

To my parents, Samson (Carrie) Ervin and Joycelyn (Walter) Henderson III, thank you for shaping my life to be who I am today. The impact you've made has been tremendous naturally and spiritually. I can never repay you for all you have done.

To all of my family and friends, thank you for your continued love and support.

When someone gets healed, the Kingdom of God is revealed, for His Kingdom is a Kingdom of wholeness, of wellbeing, and of life.
--- Billy Joe Daughtery

Prefix

I recall a children's program that aired in the late 70's and early 80's titled "Under Dog." A small dog would hear the *"save me, save me"* cry of the victimized woman, and he would soon fly announcing his grand entrance *"never fear Under Dog is here,"* then he would carry her safely to a new location.

Like the victimized women, many of us have faced many battles, be it financial hardship, physical or emotional. The believers of Christ are seeking physical, financial, emotional, and physiological healing. God's word saves us, heals us, identifies our place of discontentment and positions us safely in the Heavenly Realms, the realm inaccessible to the enemy. It is from that realm God down loads to you His will and purpose in life. God orchestrates all things be it good or bad to work together for the good of those who are called and love Him. If you are currently going through any kind of struggle. It is God's way of announcing your arrival. His method of spiritually promoting you or spiritually educating you, via life lessons. The struggle is not designed to destroy neither defeat you, what purpose would that serve? God's plan for every believer is a fulfilled purpose. He did not indicate that it would come without difficulty. On this journey there will be many test and options. The choices you make, will determine whether you win or learn in life. Ephesians 6:12 says in the heavenly realm we are seated with Him (Christ) far above every principalities, powers and rulers of the darkness of this world and wicked spirits in high places. The seat represents a place of authority. It is by God's design for humanity while standing in earth to rule from the place of authority in the heavenlies. From this realm there are no worries, nor sweating. Why? Demons and devils are not above you; they are under your feet. We have authority to tread upon all serpent's and scorpions, nothing by any means shall harm you. So I say to you, put your amour on. You don't have to fear. Jehovah Shammah, Jehovah Nisi, Jehovah Shalom, Jehovah Jireh, Jehovah Rapha, Elhay Yishi, Elohim Chaiyim and El HaNe'eman the faithful God. Is near hiding, protecting and defending. He's secured a hiding place for you that is undetectable by the enemy (Psalms 34:4). The shadow of God Almighty will become your hiding place in this season (Psalms 91:1). The sages say that Moses wrote Psalms 91 as he dwelt in the secret place of the Most High God, "in the midst of the dark cloud" (Exodus 24:18), a place of sacred and holy concealment. The thick clouds are a "hiding place" for Him (Job 22:14). Notice that the one who "abides" in the secret of the Most High dwells in an ascended place of rest- being lifted above the surrounding madness of this fallen world of flux and shadows. The Hebrew words means to lodge or to "sleep" connecting it with death and resurrection. By dwelling in the death and resurrection of God will shield you with His presence and make evil powerless before you. Since God *hides* Himself in this world (Isaiah 45:15), we must humbly seek His face to enter into the place of His holy concealment in all things. God is Elyon-High Above-but He dwell "with the lowly and the broken heart (Isaiah 57:15).Therefore the Lord our God is called Shaddai-our Sustainer, Provider, Refuge, and Home. Just as we can be surrounded by the "shadow of death" (tzal mavet) so we can be surrounded by the "shadow of Shaddai" (tzal Shaddai). Like a powerful eagle brooding over her chicks, so Shaddai covers you with wings of protection (Psalms 91:4). When you "abide" in the secret place of Elyon-The Ascended One- you are concealed by the dark clouds of God's Glory, and the Presence of Shaddai overshadows you. The Lord will save you from the ensnaring trap and from the devastating pestilence (Psalms 91:3). By abiding in the truth that God's presence pervades all things at all times-you become a "stranger" with the lord of this world, a sojourner who awaits the recompense of the wicked and the healing of the world at the end of the age.

With that being said, I present to you, *The Power to Heal.* This book is packed with revelation and strategic power pact prayers that will help you to navigate successfully in reigning in life. You will acquire the necessary tools to strengthen your faith, shift your beliefs and pray from the correct dimension to achieve victory.

The Power to Heal book will teach you how to administrate healing from the Government of Heaven. You will learn as an Ambassador of the Kingdom of God; the correct position of prayer is not standing in earth and pulling down from heaven, 2 Corinthians 10:4 speaks of "pulling down strongholds". Strongholds are destroyed when a higher force is revealed. Without revelation there will never be manifestation. The Kingdom of God is an expression of God through your life, through the realm of Government that is in the spirit world. You administrate it from your assigned governmental place in heaven while in earth. This book will awaken you to the truth. It is said an awakening is not a matter of intellect. For many intelligent people are deep in illusion. But rather awakening happens when one has an insatiable thirst to know the truth. The truth, it is an administrative process that God has given to you as a son that will reveal the kingdom of God through your life. The Kingdom is not what you do. It is who you are. As a son of God it is your covenantal right to administrate the healing power of God in earth.

⁴ When he heard this, Jesus said, "This sickness will not end in death. No, it is for God's glory so that God's Son may be glorified through it." ⁵ Now Jesus loved Martha and her sister and Lazarus. ⁶ So when he heard that Lazarus was sick, he stayed where he was two more days, ⁷ and then he said to his disciples, "Let us go back to Judea."

⁸ "But Rabbi," they said, "a short while ago the Jews there tried to stone you, and yet you are going back?"

⁹ Jesus answered, "Are there not twelve hours of daylight? Anyone who walks in the daytime will not stumble, for they see by this world's light. ¹⁰ It is when a person walks at night that they stumble, for they have no light."

¹¹ After he had said this, he went on to tell them, "Our friend Lazarus has fallen asleep; but I am going there to wake him up."

¹² His disciples replied, "Lord, if he sleeps, he will get better." ¹³ Jesus had been speaking of his death, but his disciples thought he meant natural sleep. ¹⁴ So then he told them plainly, "Lazarus is dead, ¹⁵ and for your sake I am glad I was not there, so that you may believe. But let us go to him."

[16] *Then Thomas (also known as Didymus[a]) said to the rest of the disciples, "Let us also go, that we may die with him."*

Jesus Comforts the Sisters Of Lazarus

[17] On his arrival, Jesus found that Lazarus had already been in the tomb for four days. [18] Now Bethany was less than two miles[b] from Jerusalem, [19] and many Jews had come to Martha and Mary to comfort them in the loss of their brother. [20] When Martha heard that Jesus was coming, she went out to meet him, but Mary stayed at home.

[21] "Lord," Martha said to Jesus, "if you had been here, my brother would not have died. [22] But I know that even now God will give you whatever you ask."

[23] Jesus said to her, "Your brother will rise again."

[24] Martha answered, "I know he will rise again in the resurrection at the last day."

[25] Jesus said to her, "I am the resurrection and the life. The one who believes in me will live, even though they die; [26] and whoever lives by believing in me will never die. Do you believe this?"

[27] "Yes, Lord," she replied, "I believe that you are the Messiah, the Son of God, who is to come into the world."

[28] After she had said this, she went back and called her sister Mary aside. "The Teacher is here," she said, "and is asking for you." [29] When Mary heard this, she got up quickly and went to

him. ³⁰ Now Jesus had not yet entered the village, but was still at the place where Martha had met him. ³¹ When the Jews who had been with Mary in the house, comforting her, noticed how quickly she got up and went out, they followed her, supposing she was going to the tomb to mourn there.

³² When Mary reached the place where Jesus was and saw him, she fell at his feet and said, "Lord, if you had been here, my brother would not have died."

³³ When Jesus saw her weeping, and the Jews who had come along with her also weeping, he was deeply moved in spirit and troubled. ³⁴ "Where have you laid him?" he asked.

"Come and see, Lord," they replied.

³⁵ Jesus wept.

³⁶ Then the Jews said, "See how he loved him!"

³⁷ But some of them said, "Could not he who opened the eyes of the blind man have kept this man from dying?"

Jesus Raises Lazarus from The Dead

³⁸ Jesus, once more deeply moved, came to the tomb. It was a cave with a stone laid across the entrance. ³⁹ "Take away the stone," he said.

"But, Lord," said Martha, the sister of the dead man, "by this time there is a bad odor, for he has been there four days."

⁴⁰ Then Jesus said, "Did I not tell you that if you believe, you will see the glory of God?"

⁴¹ So they took away the stone. Then Jesus looked up and said, "Father, I thank you that you have heard me. ⁴² I knew that you always hear me, but I said this for the benefit of the people standing here, that they may believe that you sent me."

⁴³ When he had said this, Jesus called in a loud voice, "Lazarus, come out!" ⁴⁴ The dead man came out, his hands and feet wrapped with strips of linen, and a cloth around his face.

Jesus said to them, "Take off the grave clothes and let him go."

You see clearly Lazarus was dead, but by the power and the authority of God the word demanded a response.

The Principle of activation is "WORDS"

The tongue has the power of Life and death, and those who love it (love to talk) will eat the fruit thereof. The saying goes "you become what you eat". Words carry what nourishes the body. Be it negative or positive. What you eat you become unified with.

When Jesus said "Lazarus comes forth", his word activated life into the molecular cells of Lazarus' and he got up. Jesus did not lay hands on Lazarus, as such no one has to lay hands on you to be healed. Again we see in another passage of scripture Jesus instructed a lame man laying by the pool of Bethesda "take up you bed and walk." **Mark 2:9** What did Jesus mean? Jesus simply meant. Forget about all the religious stuff you heard. I am not interested. This is Jesus instructing the man to not only take up his bed, but get up and walk! "O Lord, I am still impotent, and when the water moves no one will come to help me"? Many times, we simply like to talk religious nonsense.

Would we be willing to forget it all? The Lord Jesus said, "Do not talk any more, but rise, take up your bed and walk." If we will drop our religion and take Jesus' living word, we will be healed and receive life. That day the impotent man was healed. It is my belief it is religious to spend thousands of dollars chasing the healing man, when you have the man who heals with you. For God is working "in you" giving you the desire and the power to do what pleases him **Hebrews 13:21**. For it is God who works "in you" to will and to act in order to fulfill his good purpose **Philippians 2:13.** For you have already been established by God to do his purpose. What God established "IN YOU" no man nor movement can stop! By right of birth into the Kingdom you are given legal right to operate in the same divine power that raise Jesus from the dead. You are a child of God you must believe you have The Power to Heal.

Chapter 1
INTRODUCTION

For whom did Christ die for? Was it for all humanity or the elite? Some argue the belief that Christ died for the elect while others point that the death of Christ was for all mankind's healing and eternal salvation. Let's examine the latter first.

According to **John 3:16** Jesus died for all of mankind. "For God so loved the world that he gave his one and only Son, that whoever believes in him shall not perish but have eternal life.

Jesus died for the sins of the entire world, (cosmos) so as to pay for the sins of every human being who's ever lived, demonstrating the grace and love of God to the entire human race and securing the salvation of everyone who believes". The word "world" is clearly defined here, and it cannot mean the elite. The word "world" means the cosmos, not just humans.

In **John 3:16** Jesus was speaking with a scholar who asked what does it mean to be "born again" In Jesus response, he says "God loves the world", for certainly God could have said for God so love human. Instead, Jesus is talking about the entire cosmos, this includes all animals, birds, insects, dirt, clouds, stars, moon, etc. He died to bring all of the mentioned things back into divine order and alignment with his heavenly government.

Whether for the elite or all humanity. The real focus of death of Jesus should be on what was the intention of Jesus dying on the cross? Jesus died for reasons of the covenant. God deals with people in the covenant, and the blood signifies a new covenant or a new agreement with his people. That gives a specific audience and specifically Jesus died for his elect people. Those who have made the choice to follow him. Through Jesus death, he procured an eternal place of redemption in their stead.

Hebrews 9:15 "For this reason Christ is the mediator of a new covenant, that those who are called may receive the promised eternal inheritance – now that he has died as a ransom to set them free from the sins committed under the first covenant.

Scripture Reference:

He died for **ALL** (1 Timothy 2:6).
He died for **ALL MEN** (Romans 5:18; 1 Timothy 4:10).
He died for **US ALL**, for ALL OF US (Isaiah 53:6).
He died for the **UNGODLY** (Romans 5:6).
He died for **CHRIST-DENIERS** (2 Peter 2:1).
He died for **SINNERS** (Romans 5:8).
He died for **EVERY MAN** (Hebrews 2:9).
He died for **MANY** (Matthew 20:28).
He died for the **WORLD** (John 6:33,51; John 1:29 and John 3:16).
He died for the **WHOLE WORLD** (1 John 2:2).
He died for the **ENTIRE NATION** of Israel (John 11:50-51).
He died for the **CHURCH** (Ephesians 5:25).
He died for His **SHEEP** (John 10:11).
He died for **ME** (Galatians 2:20).

We all must rely on God's grace, and faith to receive the greatest miracle **(eternal life),** and understand that we receive healing by the same way, and it's a part of the finished work of grace along with salvation, paid for at the same time, with one blood. **Jeremiah 17:14** states "Heal me, O LORD, and I shall be healed; save me, and I shall be saved: for thou art my praise." God wants the world to know of His goodness {oh taste and see that the Lord is good - **Psalms. 34:8**} and experience His unfailing love. I've had the great opportunity to witness several healed of various disease, cancer, the growth of limbs, and heart palpitation. All the aforementioned miracles, are not eternal. The blind man Bartimaeus in **Mark 10:46-52**, received his sight miraculously, and followed Jesus, full of joy; but where is he now? He later died! In **Mark 1:29-31**, we learn about Simon's mother in law, who was in bed with a fever, and Jesus went to her and healed her instantly. But where is she? Is she still living? No! She later died!

Where is the woman in **Mark 5:25-34**, who was subject to bleeding for twelve years, and was miraculously healed by Jesus? Is she still around? No! She later died! Where is Lazarus of **John 11:1-45**, who was raised from the dead, after being in the tomb, for four days? He later died again!

Physical miracles are not everlasting! They only give you joy for a while, but Salvation is the greatest of all miracles! Healing miracles can only give you temporary life and happiness, but Salvation gives you abundant life; that is eternal life and joy!

Chapter 2
THE COMMISSIONING

In **Matthew 10:8**, Jesus commissioned His disciples to heal the sick, cleanse the lepers, raise the dead, cast out devils; "Freely you have received so freely give." In **Matthew 8:16**, in the region of Capernaum. Jesus healed all who were sick. **Matthew 9:35** says, "Jesus went about all the cities, and He healed every sickness, and everyone diseased."

Many of the healed didn't convert to Christ, yet He healed them all. "And whithersoever he entered, into villages, or cities, or country, they laid the sick in the streets, and besought him that they might touch if it were but the border of his garment: and as many as touched him were made whole" nothing missing, nothing broken. **Mark 6:56** KJV

In both the Old and New Testaments, the Greek word salvation is **Sozo,** meaning *health, healing, prosperity, whole, soundness, preservation and deliverance. The* greatest healing that you can receive is the healing of salvation. Receive a touch from God today and it will make you whole in every area of your life. **John 3:17, 47, Ephesians 2:8-9, Romans 10:9**. It has been proven throughout the years that the life of anyone who comes into contact with our Savior has changed for eternal for all intent and purposes.

The true Gospel of Jesus Christ is a revelation of how God has taken a sinful man and made him a new creature and imparted to him a perfect righteousness. - John Osteen

I want to clarify: sickness is not a curse from God. He became a curse so that you and I wouldn't have to **Galatians 3:13-14** "Christ hath redeemed us from the curse of the law, being made a curse for us; for it is written, cursed is every one that hangeth on a tree: That the blessings of Abraham might come on the Gentiles through Jesus Christ." **Deuteronomy 28:15-48** gives us a great example of curses that shall befall the disobedient. "*But it shall come to pass, if thou wilt not hearken unto the voice of the LORD thy God, to observe to do all his commandments and his statutes which I command thee this day; that all these curses shall come upon thee, and overtake thee: Cursed [shalt] thou [be] in the city, and cursed [shalt] thou [be] in the field.*

Cursed [shall be] thy basket and thy store. Cursed [shall be] the fruit of thy body, and the fruit of thy land, the increase of thy kine, and the flocks of thy sheep. Cursed [shalt] thou [be] when thou comest in and cursed [shalt] thou [be] when thou goest out. The LORD shall send upon thee cursing, vexation, and rebuke, in all that thou settest thine hand unto for to do, until thou be destroyed, and until thou perish quickly; because of the wickedness of thy doings, whereby thou hast forsaken me.

The LORD shall make the pestilence cleave unto thee, until he have consumed thee from off the land, whither thou goest to possess it. The LORD shall smite thee with a consumption, and with a fever, and with an inflammation, and with an extreme burning, and with the sword, and with blasting, and with mildew; and they shall pursue thee until thou perish. And thy heaven that [is] over thy head shall be brass, and the earth that is under thee [shall be] iron.

The LORD shall make the rain of thy land powder and dust: from heaven shall it come down upon thee, until thou be destroyed. The

LORD shall cause thee to be smitten before thine enemies: thou shalt go out one way against them, and flee seven ways before them: and shalt be removed into all the kingdoms of the earth. And thy carcase shall be meat unto all fowls of the air, and unto the beasts of the earth, and no man shall fray [them] away.

The LORD will smite thee with the botch of Egypt, and with the emerods, and with the scab, and with the itch, whereof thou canst not be healed. The LORD shall smite thee with madness, and blindness, and astonishment of heart: And thou shalt grope at noonday, as the blind gropeth in darkness, and thou shalt not prosper in thy ways: and thou shalt be only oppressed and spoiled evermore, and no man shall save [thee].

Thou shalt betroth a wife, and another man shall lie with her: thou shalt build an house, and thou shalt not dwell therein: thou shalt plant a vineyard, and shalt not gather the grapes thereof. Thine ox [shall be] slain before thine eyes, and thou shalt not eat thereof: thine ass [shall be] violently taken away from before thy face, and shall not be restored to thee: thy sheep [shall be] given unto thine enemies, and thou shalt have none to rescue [them]. Thy sons and thy daughters [shall be] given unto another people, and thine eyes shall look, and fail [with longing] for them all the day long: and [there shall be] no might in thine hand.

The fruit of thy land, and all thy labours, shall a nation which thou knowest not eat up; and thou shalt be only oppressed and crushed alway: So that thou shalt be mad for the sight of thine eyes which thou shalt see. The LORD shall smite thee in the knees, and in the legs, with a sore botch that cannot be healed, from the sole of thy foot unto the top of thy head.

The LORD shall bring thee, and thy king which thou shalt set over thee, unto a nation which neither thou nor thy fathers have known; and there shalt thou serve other gods, wood and stone. And thou shalt become an astonishment, a proverb, and a byword, among all nations whither the LORD shall lead thee. Thou shalt carry much seed out into the field, and shalt gather [but] little in; for the locust shall consume it. Thou shalt plant vineyards, and dress [them], but shalt neither drink [of] the wine, nor gather [the grapes]; for the worms shall eat them.

Thou shalt have olive trees throughout all thy coasts, but thou shalt not anoint [thyself] with the oil; for thine olive shall cast [his fruit]. Thou shalt beget sons and daughters, but thou shalt not enjoy them; for they shall go into captivity. All thy trees and fruit of thy land shall the locust consume. The stranger that [is] within thee shall get up above thee very high; and thou shalt come down very low. He shall lend to thee, and thou shalt not lend to him: he shall be the head, and thou shalt be the tail. Moreover all these curses shall come upon thee, and shall pursue thee, and overtake thee, till thou be destroyed; because thou hearkenedst not unto the voice of the LORD thy God, to keep his commandments and his statutes which he commanded thee:

And they shall be upon thee for a sign and for a wonder, and upon thy seed for ever. Because thou servedst not the LORD thy God with joyfulness, and with gladness of heart, for the abundance of all [things]; Therefore shalt thou serve thine enemies which the LORD shall send against thee, in hunger, and in thirst, and in nakedness, and in want of all [things]: and he shall put a yoke of iron upon thy neck, until he have destroyed thee."

Proverbs 26:2 says "Like a flitting sparrow, like a flying swallow, so a curse without cause shall not alight." - As we continue in Christ, the curse has no right to take root in our lives.

Chapter 3
SIN PUNISHMENT

Sin Punishment? What am I expressing? I encourage you not to buy into the deception sickness is God's way of punishing you for sin **Romans 8:2** states "for the law of the spirit of life in Christ Jesus has made me free from the law of sin and death." *And the effects of death and the curse!* Jesus' disciples asked him, **John 9: 2-3** "Rabbi, who sinned, this man or his parents that he was born blind?" "Neither this man nor his parents sinned," said Jesus, "but this happened so that the work of God might be displayed in his life." Sickness and disease are from the devil. He comes to steal, kill, and destroy. Our Father doesn't have to prove how powerful He is through sickness. God has always been a lover He does not use fear, sickness or any other tactic as a penalty for sin.

Our belief that God uses sickness as a punishment for sin is not biblical. There is a famous saying that, "Jesus paid a debt He did not owe, to cancel a debt He did not pay." The penalty for sin was already paid for in full at the cross. When Jesus said, "It is finished!" He was not kidding. He took the punishment of our sin, and our iniquity in His own body.

Think about all that Jesus suffered. Would He have endured so much, if His plan was to use sickness to punish us, who are sinners?

Romans 6:23 says, "For the wages of sin is death, but the gift of God is eternal life." The wages have been paid. We don't owe sin anything. So why do we think we have to pay for our sin, through sickness?

Jesus came that we might have life. **1 Peter 2:24**, "He himself bore our sins in his body on the cross, so we might die to sins and live for righteousness, 'by his wounds you have been healed.'"

Chapter 4
THE MIND HEALS

There is an age old saying that 'belief's kill, and belief cures.' This is something that has been experimented with for centuries, and science confirms it to some extent. Studies have been done with what they call 'placebos.' A placebo is defined as, *"a medicine or procedure prescribed for the psychological benefit to the patient rather than for any physiological effect....a substance that has no therapeutic effect, used as a control in testing new drugs... a measure designed merely to humour or placate someone."* Patients have been given a placebo to take overtime for various symptoms, and they are told what it will do, when in reality, the medications have no more value than a tic tac, yet the results have been phenomenal. Symptoms disappear simply because the patient believes that what they are taking will alleviate symptoms.

I find it interesting that Scientist have laid the bible aside for centuries, and taken the long road to determine what life is, only to find that their discoveries are already written in the Word.

"Everything is possible for one who believes." **St. Mark 9:23 – NIV**

Faith is to be fully persuaded in your mind of a fact. In the same way that you put confidence in the medication you are given, even if it's a placebo, and you experience favorable results, if you can put that same faith in God, all things become possible, including healing from any infirmity.

Amazingly, we have built a culture where we are more comfortable putting our confidence in medication, and bad diagnosis, than in God's Word. We have somehow convinced ourselves that God needs help to heal us. We live what we believe. Whatever our minds accept as truth, will be the reality we walk in. Have you ever looked at the ingredients they put in medication? Have you ever researched some of the components to see where they come from, or what was its original purpose? Putting faith in medicine is as risky as trusting God. Here what David says:

It is better to trust in the LORD than to put confidence in man. **Psalm 118:8 – KJV**

Solomon says:

Trust in the LORD with all your heart and lean not on your own understanding; **Proverbs 3:5 – NIV**

I find that trust and faith is a condition of the mind. If you are not convinced in your mind, that will or can hinder your healing. To be healed, we have to be fully convinced in our minds that God will heal us.

And without faith it is impossible to please God, because anyone who comes to him must believe that he exists and that he rewards those who earnestly seek him. **Hebrews 11:6 – NIV**

The mind is a powerful thing. Every religion knows this to be truly. Have you ever spoken to somehow who is fully convinced in their mind of a very obvious lie? No wonder Paul says:

Do not conform to the pattern of this world, but be transformed by the renewing of your mind. Then you will be able to test and approve what God's will is--his good, pleasing and perfect will. **Romans 12:2 – NIV**

Our transformation as children of God is tied to a renewed mind. You can be saved, and your mind is un-renewed. I believe this is the major reason some people are not healed, our prayers go unanswered, we experience lack and even when healing comes, it last but a moment.

Science believes you can heal yourself with your mind. What they are actually purporting is simply how God created us initially. If you can tap into the full capacity of the mind, you can experience healing with or without God. It's just how we are designed, and the enemy knows this. We are supernatural beings, made to function like a supernatural being.

Look at the story of the tower of babel. Men came together with one 'mind' to build a tower into the heavens. God had to intervene and stop them, or they would have succeeded. Hear what God said:

And the LORD said, Behold, the people *is* one, and they have all one language; and this they begin to do: and now nothing will be restrained from them, which they have ***imagined*** to do. **Genesis 11:6 – KJV**

They were accomplishing this feat without God. The idea started at an image in their minds. They saw themselves doing it, and they acted on it.

Healing takes place in very much the same way. You take God's reality and make it your reality:

Surely he took up our pain and bore our suffering, yet we considered him punished by God, stricken by him, and afflicted. But he was pierced for our transgressions, he was crushed for our iniquities; the punishment that brought us peace was on him, and by his wounds we are healed. **Isaiah 53:4-5 – NIV**

When you grab a hold of the truth, you have to hold that image in your mind. If you were confined to a wheelchair, you begin to see yourself walking in your mind. You accept the truth of God's Word over your present reality. Benny Hinn once made a statement, "You will be healed when Jesus is more real to you than your sickness."

A renewed mind is a mind that heals. But what does a renewed mind look like? How do we renew our minds, when we are in need of divine healing?

Our minds are renewed through the Word:

How can a young person stay on the path of purity? By living according to your word. <u>Psalm 119:9</u>

Whatever the Word says, that you do.

This book of the law shall not depart out of thy mouth; but thou shalt meditate therein day and night, that thou mayest observe to do according to all that is written therein: for then thou shalt make thy way prosperous, and then thou shalt have good success. <u>Joshua 1:8</u>

To meditate means you roll it over and over in your mind, like a cow chewing on his cud.

Husbands, love your wives, just as Christ loved the church and gave himself up for her to make her holy, cleansing her by the <u>washing with water through the word</u>, and to present her to himself as a radiant church, without stain or wrinkle or any other blemish, but holy and blameless. <u>Ephesians 5:25-27</u>

So, the Word of God plays a vital role in the renewing process. Whatever you read, whatever you watch, whatever you listen to goes into your soul, goes into your mind and forms a pattern of thinking....and that pattern will either reflect the world, or it will reflect the kingdom of God. If you are believing for healing, you need to fill your mind with healing scriptures, and testimonies of healing.

It is from this place that we speak, so you can usually tell the spiritual state of someone, or even discern their heart from what they say, especially when you live with a renewed mind...you can easily discern anger, bitterness, resentment, offense, etc.

One other way to continually renew your mind is to apply the blood of Jesus to your mind:

And they overcame him by the blood of the Lamb, and by the word of their testimony; and they loved not their lives unto the death. **Revelation 12:11**

Chapter 5
WHAT'S EATING YOU

The world, predominantly, influences today what we eat, but we need to be mindful of the fact that before there was a world system, there was only a God system.

I often look back at the brief recorded life of Adam and Eve as an indication about how we should live as born again Christians: We eat what God says we are to eat.

Then God said, "I give you every seed-bearing plant on the face of the whole earth and every tree that has fruit with seed in it. They will be yours for food. **Genesis 1:29 – NIV**

Initially, that was what man was commissioned to eat. I assume as well that what was made as food for man, had all that the man needed in terms of nutrition and maintaining health.

It was after the flood, in Noah's day, that God allowed man to start eating meat:

"All the animals, birds, and fish will live in fear of you. They are all placed under your power. Now you can eat them, as well as green plants; I give them all to you for food. The one thing you must not eat is meat with blood still in it; I forbid this because the life is in the blood." **Genesis 9:2-4** – Good News Bible

In my humble opinion, the world has taken a long trip around the wilderness, only to find themselves back at the original place. I also believe that God is taking us back to the very origins of creation, as it relates to maintaining health through a balanced meal.

God created us, so surely He knows how to sustain us. Apart from the gift of having Holy Spirit lives in us, there is an added responsibility to treat our temples right:

Know ye not that your bodies are the members of Christ? shall I then take the members of Christ, and make them the members of an harlot? God forbid. What? know ye not that he which is joined to an harlot is one body? for two, saith he, shall be one flesh. But he that is joined unto the Lord is one spirit. **1 Corinthians 6:15-20 – NIV**

We have not been doing well in terms of what we put into God's temple. We see the passion that Jesus displayed over the physical temple that should have been considered the house of prayer, yet it was desecrated by what it was being used for; a marketplace. They weren't selling anything bad. They were trading the normal stuff people would be using for the daily sacrifice, and yet it was greeted with holy anger from the Lord.

We have to take care in what we put into God's temple.

I titled this Chapter "What Is Eating You" even though I am addressing what we eat. The truth is, what you eat, may be doing more harm to you than good, in essence, what you are putting into your body is eating away your health, strength and vitality.

I have never seen so many sick people in all my life. It seems everyone is struggling with some ailment, or the other. You would think in a technologically advanced world, with all the breakthrough procedures, medications, and treatments, that the population would be getting healthier, but what we see is the complete opposite.

Instead of trusting your health into the hands of another man, you may want to consider your options.

Stop trusting in mere humans, who have but a breath in their nostrils. Why hold them in esteem? **Isaiah 2:22 – NIV**

A recent article published on foodkills.org recently states:

At the beginning of the 20th century the US ranked 1st in health among the major industrial nations. US spending per capita on health is currently the highest in the world yet the US now ranks 37th in actual health statistics in the top industrial countries and has the highest infant mortality rate. The US also rates 24th in life expectancy. So what happened in the last century to cause this dramatic reversal? This website will detail the exact causes of this breakdown in American health. It doesn't take a rocket scientist to realize that there is something seriously wrong with the current medical model which mostly consists of suppressing symptoms rather than finding true causes. But there's more to it than that. If you look into the field of natural alternative cures, especially nutrition, you can be immediately struck by the fact that it is a very confused field full of contrary data. You can read books extolling the virtues of various herbs or minerals and then books warning of the harm from the exact same substances. Some books promote eating certain foods and others recommend avoiding those same foods. You can see a lot of fads and a mixture of seemingly sensible ideas and some quite bizarre ones.

Man's attempt to play god is failing miserably. It was never Gods intention to trust the health to man into the hands of men. If we are careful to obey His laws, says the Lord, He would not allow disease to come upon us.

So, now we must take a radical, and conscious approach to our health, and be mindful of what we put into our bodies.

Foods, for the most part, is being genetically modified as men attempt to make food last longer on shelves, etc.

If you can recall, the children of Israel was fed manna in the wilderness. God provided their daily portions and told them not to leave any for the next day, except for the Sabbath. Man's attempt to change this has resulted in genetically modified foods (GMO's) full of preservatives and chemicals that do far more harm than good. Even our fruits and vegetables are being genetically modified. This information would make you almost paranoid to put anything in your mouth.

There is good news. God wants to re-establish a healthy community, a vibrant body of people, a glorious church on the foundation of a relationship with Him. Our health will flow from our times spent in His presence where He will instruct us on what to eat, and what to do to take care of the temple in which He now dwells.

Both sin and sickness came into the world through the fall of the human race. Therefore, we must look for the healing of both in the savior of the human race. God is as willing to heal believers as He is to forgive unbelievers. Know this; if He was merciful enough to forgive you when you were unconverted, He is merciful enough to heal you now that you are in His family! - T. L. Osborn

Chapter 6
HEALING OF THE SOUL

Beloved, I wish above all things that thou mayest prosper and be in health, even as thy soul prospereth. **3 John 1:2 – KJV**

As I followed Jesus Ministry throughout the New Testament, I often wondered why while healing someone, He would say, "Be made whole."

And when they were gone over, they came into the land of Gennesaret. And when the men of that place had knowledge of him, they sent out into all that country round about, and brought unto him all that were diseased; And besought him that they might only touch the hem of his garment: and as many as touched were made perfectly whole. **St. Matthew 14:34-36 – KJV**

Jesus was not just healing the physical body, and casting out demons, but He was making those who came to him 'Whole'.

In the last decade or so, there has been a release of understanding of the human soul, and how it functions and its true nature. This understanding is needed to be able to properly interpret that scripture that troubles many of us in **3 John 1:2**, "I wish above all that you prosper and be in good health..." This has been challenging to accept as God's will, because most people are sick, and not very prosperous. But there is a clause, "...even as your soul prospers." What does it mean for our souls to prosper, or even for us to be made whole?

Ana Mendez believes that our souls can be fragmented. What this practically means is, due to trauma, or a number of things, a part of us can be separated and even held in what she calls "Regions Of Captivity." She describes a part of our soul as a transparent version of ourselves, so it looks like us. She has been delivering these fragmented souls, and uniting them, making a person whole again, and have seen miraculous things happen because of this. She calls this "High Level Warfare."

Kat Kerr says she has seen the human soul. It is made up of layers, and each layer is a full transparent version of the person. She likens the soul to the Holy Spirit who is able to deposit a full version of Himself in each individual Believer.

These thoughts enlighten us to the reality of who we are. Humanity has been studying the human body for many years. But they have no idea who we are, in terms of being soul and spirit. How does the soul relate to the body? What relations do they have?

There are now ministers who specialize in the healing of the soul. They believe that sickness can be a result of wounds that we have received in our soul. How is the soul wounded? A broken heart, trauma, sexual abuse, and sin.

Sickness does not originate in the body. It never has, and I believe this is why medicine can only alleviate symptoms, but it cannot heal the wounds in our souls. There is no prescription for soul scars, except the blood of Jesus.

I met a young woman once who was almost crippled. She was thin, and her body twisted, her feet twisted and she seemed to struggle to walk. We started a conversation. She had found a video on youtube about healing the soul, and begun to pray that prayer every day. She says her condition has been improving daily ever since.

Our bodies reproduce what is hidden in our souls, and this sometimes manifest itself as sickness, especially chronic sicknesses, as phobia's or mental issues. In order to heal our bodies, we must first be healed in our souls.

When the righteous cry for help, the LORD hears and delivers them out of all their troubles. The LORD is near to the brokenhearted and saves the crushed in spirit. Many are the afflictions of the righteous, but the LORD delivers him out of them all. He keeps all his bones; not one of them is broken. **Psalm 34:17-20 – ESV**

God wants to make you whole. Because we are complex beings, there is more to us than just healing in our bodies. For the healing to manifest in our physical bodies, the true source of what we are experiencing must be addressed. When Jesus healed, He didn't just take care of their symptoms, but He also addressed their sins, and the consequences. This 'wholeness' is what He desires for you, and when we achieve this, then we will prosper and be in good health.

He restores my soul. He leads me in paths of righteousness for his name's sake. **(Psalm 23:3)**

Chapter 7
EMOTIONAL HEALING

Create in me a clean heart, O God, and renew a right spirit within me. <u>Psalm 51:10 – ESV</u>

Many are suffering today from emotional problems leading to anxiety, depression, PTSD, etc. There are so many people who go to doctors because of symptoms they are experiencing in their bodies, but the doctors cannot find anything wrong with them. They spend a lot of money running test, and trying different medications, only to find minimal relief from their suffering. The fact is, in many of these cases what is needed is emotional healing. This goes in conjunction with the healing of the soul, but still deserves a place of its own in this book.

There is one particular emotional trauma that seems to be very common among the general population. There are many books written about the subject, and also there may be some demonization associated with the trauma, but not everyone suffering needs deliverance from evil spirits. It is important to walk in the Spirit, and be led by the Spirit in addressing these issues. We cannot minimize the importance of the gift of discernment in this case.

The emotional trauma of sexual abuse can affect a person all their life. Even with years of counselling, on many occasion the effect is not minimized, nor a remedy applied. This is one thing you can't put a band aid on, but need to experience the power of the cross.

Sexual abuse is unwanted sexual activity, with perpetrators using force, making threats or taking advantage of victims not able to give consent. Most victims and perpetrators know each other. Immediate reactions to sexual abuse include shock, fear or disbelief. Long-term symptoms include anxiety, fear or post-traumatic stress disorder. While efforts to treat sex offenders remain unpromising, psychological interventions for survivors — especially group therapy — appears effective. [1]

You would be surprised to know that there are people who know who have been dealing with emotional trauma is this area. Many suffer in silence, not having anyone they can open up to and the effects are far reaching. There are so many families, marriages that have been seriously impacted by this. When your emotions are damaged by trauma, it is hard for you to function at your maximum potential.

Ana Mendez believes that in some cases like this, a layer of your soul is held in regions of captivity, where it relives the moment over and over again. In some cases, when such a person is to receive healing or deliverance in this area, there is a need to go back to the exact place and time when it took place. If you should see that fragmented soul, even though the person may be an adult, that version of themselves is the same age as the time the abuse took place.

---

[1]   Encyclopaedia of Psychology

Joyce Myers have been working with abused women for years. She notes that even though God wants to heal emotional, there are some steps that an individual has to take for themselves.

1. Face the truth. There is no freedom in living in denial, and pretending that some things never happened. They did, and you must be ready to face up to it. There is no darkness that can persist when dragged into the light.
2. Confession. When we are willing to confess our faults, we become a testimony in progress. We have to be accountable to each other, and there is always someone that we can trust, who we open up to. How can we effectively pray for each other, if we don't know what we are praying for? Confession is not unloading your burden on someone else's shoulder, but exposing yourself to accountability.
3. Assume Personal Responsibility. There is no sense in living in denial, and being afraid to revisit your past. For you to be whole, you must deal with those issues in your past. You will know that you are whole when you can talk about your past, and it doesn't bother you anymore. You may even feel like you are talking about somebody else. This is when your testimony becomes a weapon against the enemy, to the point of liberating others.

So, the first step to your healing is being willing to admit that you have an issue. Facing the truth is the beginning of a happier life.

Emotional healing is something that every person needs, to one degree or another, for we have all been wounded emotionally.

There are many variations of emotional brokenness and pain—as many as there are types of people. Whether the cause is natural or because of another's sin, the majority of people fight some type of emotional battle. [2]

God wants to restore your soul **Psalm 23:3.** Jesus came to heal the brokenhearted **St. Luke 4:18.** Healing is a process that involves moment by moment choices to trust and obey God. We must choose healthy interactions with others **1 Peter 3:8-12,** healthy thinking based on the truth of scripture **Philippians 4:4-9** and engage in healthy activities that benefit our bodies **2 Corinthians 7:1.**

Take time out of our day to meditate on God's word. **Proverbs 4:22** says, it is "...life to those who find them and health to one's whole body." Here are some additional scriptures to meditate on, **Psalm 73:23-26; Psalm 34:17-20; 1 Peter 5:7; Psalm 147:3; Psalm 30:11; John 14:27; Matthew 11:28; Romans 5:1;** and **Romans 8:32.**

Take control of your thoughts. **2 Corinthians 10:5** says, "...we take captive every thought to make it obedient to Christ."

Forgive those who have hurt you. This is very important, though it may prove to be extremely hard to do. **Ephesians 4:32** says, "Be kind and compassionate to one another, forgiving each other, just as in Christ, God forgave you." Unforgiveness fosters a root of bitterness in the soul, and this can make you very sick in your bodies.

---

[2]   http://www.gotquestions.org/emotional-healing.html

Chapter 8
GOD'S REDEMPTIVE PLAN.

Jesus' death wasn't the result of sin, sickness or disobedience. His death was God's redemption plan for man's eternal salvation. As a result, all things were made new, you are redeemed, you are healed, and you are delivered from unclean spirits. You don't have to wait until you are in heaven to walk in the fullness of the salvation *(health, healing, prosperity, wholeness, soundness, preservation and deliverance)* of God. It is not the Father's will that any man should perish but to have access to everything the government of the Kingdom of Heaven has to offer, right now, right here, in the earth.

You may think that God's redemptive plan came into fruition when Adam and Eve sinned, but that was not the inception of this divine, and glorious rescue. **Revelation 13:8** says, "All inhabitants of the earth will worship the beast – all whose names have not been written in the Lamb's book of life, the Lamb who was slain from the creation of the world."

God had a plan before He breathe His breathe into the nostrils of Adam. He knew humanity would fall, and He knew that it was His life that would be given at the hands of His own creation to save them. But why such a heavy sacrifice? **Leviticus 17:11** gives us a shadow, "For the life of a creature is in the blood, and I have given it to you to make atonement for yourselves on the altar; it is the blood that makes atonement for one's life."

Before Jesus came, the church made sacrifices according to the Mosaic law, but it was clear that the blood of animals did nothing to change the heart of men, and it is such a change of heart that is referred to as repentance. There was only one blood type that could truly atone for man's sin, and open a gateway for his heart to be cleansed, and the law of God to be written on it.

Jesus was and is God the Father's redemptive plan from the very beginning of creation. In God's eyes, humanity has already been redeemed. It is for us, individually, to step into the full reality of what that means, and that involves reigning with Jesus Christ on the earth, and for all eternity.

Romans 5:17 "For if by the one man's offense [Adam] death reigned through the one, much more those who receive abundance of grace and of the gift of righteousness **will reign in life** through the one, Jesus Christ." This verse doesn't speak of the past tense or future hope we should look forward to in heaven. It guarantees that we will reign in this life right here, and now. Are you reigning or being rained on?

The reality of the cross is a restoration of what was lost during the fall. The promise of God was that mankind would be redeemed, which means our original mandate is still valid, "...subdue the earth, and rule..." **Genesis 1:28**. The dominion of the earth was given to man. It is a position we lost when we sinned. Jesus came, as the full embodiment of who Adam was, before the fall, to pave a path for anyone who would believe in Him to walk this path.

The dominion, and authority that Jesus exercised over demons, sickness and poverty is embedded within us, and limited only by our knowledge of who we are in Him.

"I can do all things through Christ, who gives me strength" **Philippians 4:13** is not a cliché. The reason most of us function below our inherited capacity, is because we cannot operate above the level of our faith. The fact is, is you truly believe you can walk on water, you will. Jesus has removed all limitations through His life and ministry on earth.

There is an open invitation to every believer to reign with Christ. Paul says in **2 Timothy 2:12**, "If we endure hardship, we will reign with him. If we deny him, He will deny us."

I think one of our hindrances to reigning is our inability to endure difficulties, yet that is the path into the kingdom of God. We see this in **Acts 14:22**, "...We must go through many hardships to enter the kingdom of God."

This is the same path that Jesus took, and He became the door. He refers to the path as narrow, but it is the only true way to enter. He also mentioned that there are some who enter by a different way, but He calls them thieves and robbers.

You don't have to be burdened down by the cares of this life. You don't have to be sick, and depleted; broke and in debt; or living under a curse. Jesus enables you to rise and live above all this. **Ephesians 2:6** says, "And God raised us up with Christ and seated us with Him in the heavenly realms in Christ Jesus" which simply means that your true position is seated **Ephesians 1:21** Far above all principality, and power, and might, and dominion, and every name that is named, not only in this world, but also in that which is to come.

There Is a Higher Government Who Looks at Earth For Its Shadow.

The Kingdom of Heaven is where the government of God sits. The government of God is set up as our judicial earthly legal system. The judiciary (also known as the judicial system or court system) is the system of courts that interprets and applies the law in the name of the state. Thus the government of God established in three's, God the Father, God the Son, and God the Holy Spirit is the domain of God that exists inside of you. The kingdom of God is within you. God has chosen you to become an expression of Him on the face of the earth. **Luke 17:21** Why is it important for the earth to look like heaven? God has a will. Thy kingdom come thy will be done in earth. **Matthew 6:10** Jesus said "Father if it is your will, take this cup from me, but not my will let thy will be done on earth. **Luke 24:42**. He wants the earth to look just like heaven. There is no darkness in heaven, no form of pain. God desires that all kind of darkness **(i.e. pain, sickness, habitual sin)** to be done away with so that the government of heaven would rule on earth just like it is in heaven. What is the government of heaven? It is the spiritual governing from the realm of heaven that administrates the will of the Father on earth.

We are told that we can have heaven on Earth. That when we pray with strength and power heaven invades earth. We are also told that God has everything we need in the heavens. This is true, the full supply of God's provisions for you is as close to you as the air you breathe. Your physical healing is close, your financial healing is close, and physiological healing is close. When you engage the heavenly realm, you can achieve whatever thing you need on earth. It's about an administrative process that God has given us that will reveal the kingdom through our lives. The kingdom is not what you do (casting out devils, healing etc, these are gifts, signs, and wonders to display the kingdom) God wants His kingdom revealed through you, you are the transporter of his Kingdom entering earth.

Ephesians 1:3 says, "Praise be to the God and Father of our Lord Jesus Christ, who has blessed us in the heavenly realms with every spiritual blessing in Christ." Do you know what our real responsibility as children of God is? We are supposed to take what we see in heaven, and reproduce it here. Jesus says, "...Very truly I tell you, the Son can do nothing by himself; he can do only what he **sees** his Father doing, because whatever the Father does the Son also does." **St. John 5:19** If we are to be like Jesus, and do what He did, and greater things, our ability to see is very important. How else will we do what Paul says, "Imitate God, therefore, in everything you do, because you are His dear children."

If earth is ever to begin to look like heaven, then we need to know and see what heaven is like. We need to know what the Father is doing in any given moment. I believe this is the key to miracles. Jesus seldom healed any two people the same way. He had to be directly connected to God to see how best He should minister to those who came to Him, and He was always right. We get it wrong sometimes.

Heaven on earth is all about facilitating a culture where God's will override all other 'wills.' Jesus said, in the Garden of Gethsemane, "...not MY will, but YOUR will be done." We pray this as well in the Lord's prayer, "Thy will be done on earth, as it is in heaven." Our citizenship is in heaven; we are ambassadors of heaven; we are seated in heavenly places; the kingdom of God is within us; we have Holy Spirit...heaven on earth should be our daily reality.

Chapter 9
LEGAL CONTRACT

Victory in life should be common in the household of every believer. If you're not experiencing victory, know that there is a breach in your contract with Christ. **1 John 15:14** states "And if we know that he hears us, whatsoever we ask, we know that we have the petitions that we desired of him." The word *petition* in this verse means a legal contract or binding agreement between two parties. God cannot and will not break His word. His word became legal and binding when he stated "let them" giving (man) legal authority on the earth to subdue and have dominion over every living thing as mentioned in **Genesis 1:28** that includes cancer, bacteria, parasites, viruses and all microorganisms that cause sickness and disease. He gave the blessing, He gave the command, and He gave **you** the right.

Today we have heard stories and even witness this legal contract appears to not be very binding in the life of many Christians who struggle with questions arising from these scriptures:

St. Matthew 18:19 – Again I say to you, if two of you agree on earth about anything they ask, it will be done for them by my Father in heaven."

<u>St. Matthew 21:22</u> - "And whatever you ask in prayer, you will receive, if you have faith."

<u>St. Mark 11:24</u> - "Therefore I tell you, whatever you ask in prayer, believe that you have received it, and it will be yours."

<u>St. John 14:13</u> - "Whatever you ask in my name, this I will do, that the Father may be glorified in the Son."

<u>St. John 15:7</u> - "If you abide in me, and my words abide in you, ask whatever you wish, and it will be done for you."

And my personal favorite, <u>St. John 16:23-24</u> "In that day you will ask nothing of me. Truly, truly, I say to you, whatever you ask of the Father in my name, He will give it to you. Until now you have asked nothing in my name. Ask, and you will receive, that your joy may be full."

A very popular, mega church Pastor once said that God literally, "left Himself vulnerable" when He uttered these words repeatedly. The fact is, God is no liar, so whatever He says, that is exactly what He will do. And if the terms of the contract involve Him answering every prayer you pray, and request made, then you can live in the expectation that what you are believing for, will manifest.

Every contract has terms, and on many occasions, your participation in the process is called for. What I found absolutely profound is that God linked our joy to answered prayers. Is it no wonder so many people are depressed? Many have said, they have not seen any of the promises materialize in their own life. They have been asking, and asking, but no response. Have you ever been at that place?

God says if we seek Him, we will find Him, but the conditions are to seek Him with all our hearts, souls and minds. There has to be an agreement in your total man, for the promises of God to manifest. The kingdom of God is established on a foundation of agreement. First, your body, soul and spirit, and then connect with at least one other who is also in agreement: body, soul and spirit. It is under these conditions that we will experience the fullness of this divine contract.

Acts 2:1-2, "When the day of Pentecost came, they were all together in one place. Suddenly, a sound like the blowing of a violent wind came from heaven and filled the whole house where they were sitting."

Acts 4:23-24;31, "On their release, Peter and John went back to their own people and reported all that the chief priests and the elders had said to them. When they heard this, they raised their voices together in prayer to God. After they prayed, the place where they were meeting was shaken. And they were all filled with the Holy Spirit and spoke the word of God boldly."

It would seem that there is no body of believers that have experienced this level of unity and manifestations since the early church. When we get to this place, every word that leaves our mouth will manifest something, because that is the contract made between God and us, and signed by the blood of Jesus, in His Name.

The enemy has come to rob the church of its joy. To the world Christians appear to be the most miserable people in earth. Many have patent the artistry and invite others to join in. Everything is bad. No, it is not as bad as it appears, believe someone has it worse than you. When you turn your focus from it being about you, will you experience the joy of the Lord as your strength. Drink of Him! He will give you overflowing unspeakable joy. God is called the spirit of joy. The fruit (evidence) of the spirit is joy! C.S. Lewis said joy is the serious business of heaven. Your joy is heavens business. It brings God pleasure to bring you joy. If you follow joy to its fullest you will discover, God is right there. I pray as you pray the prayer of renewal below that you experience the intoxicating joy of the Lord and may it be infectious among those whom you come in contact.

Pray of Renewal:

Father, today I renew my covenant with you. I want to be one with you and one with your Spirit.

1. Father you said in your word. With long life I shall be satisfied, I want that.
2. You said he who eats your body and drink your blood shall never die, Father I want that.
3. You said all the silver and all the gold is yours, Father I want some silver and gold.
4. You said no plague shall come nigh my dwelling, Father I want that.
5. You said you will give me an abundance of wealth, Father I want that.

6. You said my cup shall run over, Father I want that.
7. You said I am blessed going in and blessed going out, Father I want that.
8. Father I want you to meet me every time I enter into your presence.
9. Father I want your presence to hover over me like a tent daily.
10. Father you said all that I shall lay my hands on shall prosper, I want that.
11. Father you said those who know their God shall be strong and do great exploits, Father I want to be strong and do great exploits in you.
12. Father you said I shall dwell in the good of the land, Father I want that.
13. Father I want to see heaven with my eyes.
14. Father I want your angels and men in white linen to accompany me daily.
15. Father I want Holy Spirit to dwell thickly among me.

Chapter 10
IGNORANCE THE GREATEST WEAPON

The word of God doesn't state that people perish from sickness or disease. On the contrary, it says that people perish because of a lack of knowledge.

Hosea 4:6- My people are destroyed for lack of knowledge: because thou hast rejected knowledge, I will also reject thee, that thou shalt be no priest to me: seeing thou hast forgotten the law of thy God, I will also forget thy children.

Mariam Webster defines knowledge as facts, information, and skills acquired by a person through experience or education; the theoretical or practical understanding of a subject.

It is said that knowledge is power. I say knowledge that is exercised appropriately harnesses power. It is not enough to have a lot of information without understanding of its proper use. Knowledge puffs up; but love (spirit) gives life. **1 Corinthian 8:1**

If you have knowledge only, it will lead to pride, for knowledge alone puffs up. Like the proud Pharisee, we will gather our intellectual robes about us and pray, "God, I thank thee that I am not like other men, ignorant, uneducated, without knowledge of Barth, Brunner, and Bultmann, or even like this colporteur. Paul says, "If I have prophetic powers, and understand all mysteries and all knowledge . . . but have not love, I gain nothing" **1 Corinthians 13:2**.

Knowledge without love leads to pride of intellect, but knowledge with love leads to humility and a sense of obligation. Paul was willing to accommodate himself to the level of his hearers in order that he might win them to the gospel. He went down to their level that he might bring them up to his level.

The most freighting statement one can quote is "ignorance is bliss", what you don't know you don't worry about. Ignorance has the effect of death generationally. Global Research says: Ignorance is pervasive in America; it affects the rich as well as the poor, the powerful and the powerless, the famous as well as the obscure. It's prevalent in the suites of our nation's CEOs, the Congress, the military, and even our universities. It defines this nation.

> *"Five percent of the people think; ten percent of the people think they think; and the other eighty-five percent would rather die than think."- Thomas Edison*

Some religious sects, have it hard believing that Jesus was a real man who lived to die for the sins of humanity:

For I have come down from heaven not to do my will but to do the will of him who sent me. **John 6:38**

What did Jesus come to do?

1. **To reveal the Father (Matthew 11:27)**
   1. "All things have been committed to me by my Father. No one knows the Son except the Father, and no one knows the Father except the Son and those to whom the Son chooses to reveal him."

2. **To be a ransom for many (Matthew 20:28)**
   1. "Just as the Son of Man did not come to be served, but to serve, and to give his life as a ransom for many."

3. **To serve (Matthew 20:28)**
   1. "Just as the Son of Man did not come to be served, but to serve, and to give his life as a ransom for many."

4. **To save the world (John 3:17; Luke 19:10)**
   1. "For God did not send his Son into the world to condemn the world, but to save the world through him."

5. **To preach the good news of the kingdom of God (Luke 4:43)**
   1. "But he said, "I must preach the good news of the kingdom of God to the other towns also, because that is why I was sent."

6. **To bring division (Luke 12:51)**
   1. "Do you think I came to bring peace on earth? No, I tell you, but division."

7. **To do the will of the Father (John 6:38)**
    1. "For I have come down from heaven not to do my will but to do the will of him who sent me."

8. **To give the Father's words (John 17:8)**
    1. "For I gave them the words you gave me and they accepted them. They knew with certainty that I came from you, and they believed that you sent me."

9. **To testify to the truth (John 18:37)**
    1. "You are a king, then!" said Pilate. Jesus answered, "You are right in saying I am a king. In fact, for this reason I was born, and for this I came into the world, to testify to the truth. Everyone on the side of truth listens to me."

10. **To die and destroy Satan's power (Hebrew 2:14)**
    1. "Since the children have flesh and blood, he too shared in their humanity so that by his death he might destroy him who holds the power of death--that is, the devil."

11. **To destroy the devil's works (1 John 3:8)**
    1. "He who does what is sinful is of the devil, because the devil has been sinning from the beginning. The reason the Son of God appeared was to destroy the devil's work."

12. **To fulfill the Law and the Prophets (Matthew 5:17)**
    1. "Do not think that I have come to abolish the Law or the Prophets; I have not come to abolish them but to fulfill them."

THE POWER TO HEAL

13. To give life (John 10:10,28)

    1. "The thief comes only to steal and kill and destroy; I have come that they may have life, and have it to the full . . . I give them eternal life, and they shall never perish; no one can snatch them out of my hand."

14. To taste death for everyone (Hebrew 2:9)

    1. "But we see Jesus, who was made a little lower than the angels, now crowned with glory and honor because he suffered death, so that by the grace of God he might taste death for everyone."

15. To become a high priest (Hebrew 2:17)

    1. "For this reason he had to be made like his brothers in every way, in order that he might become a merciful and faithful high priest in service to God, and that he might make atonement for the sins of the people."

16. To atone for sin (Hebrew 2:17)

    1. "For this reason he had to be made like his brothers in every way, in order that he might become a merciful and faithful high priest in service to God, and that he might make atonement for the sins of the people."

17. To proclaim freedom for believers (Luke 4:18)

    1. "The Spirit of the Lord is on me, because he has anointed me to preach good news to the poor. He has sent me to proclaim freedom for the prisoners

and recovery of sight for the blind, to release the oppressed."

18. **To proclaim the year of the Lord's favor (Luke 4:19)**
    1. "To proclaim the year of the Lord's favor."

19. **To bring judgment (John 9:39)**
    1. "Jesus said, "For judgment I have come into this world, so that the blind will see and those who see will become blind."

20. **To take away sin (1 John 3:5)**
    1. "But you know that he appeared so that he might take away our sins. And in him is no sin."

21. **To preach (Mark 1:38)**
    1. "Jesus replied, 'Let us go somewhere else--to the nearby villages--so I can preach there also. That is why I have come.'"

22. **To call sinners (Mark 2:17)**
    1. "On hearing this, Jesus said to them, 'It is not the healthy who need a doctor, but the sick. I have not come to call the righteous, but sinners.'"

23. **To know who is true (1 John 5:20)**
    1. "We know also that the Son of God has come and has given us understanding, so that we may know him who is true. And we are in him who is true-- even in his Son Jesus Christ. He is the true God and eternal life."

"Any formal attack on ignorance is bound to fail because the masses are always ready to defend their most precious possession - their ignorance." – <u>Hendrik Willem van Loon</u>

John 1:2 records Jesus' prayer for all of His children to live a prosperous and healthy life. His will and plan from the very beginning was given to us through Adam in the Garden of Eden. Eden is a pleasure spot a place reserved just for you and I. It is Gods atmosphere. The atmosphere of Eden is not to control me but dictate what happens in my environment. I can have my own Eden because I can cultivate the presence of God anywhere. God put Adam in earth to cultivate the garden not earth. Satan wants the atmosphere so he can mess up the natural and spiritual environment with sickness and disease – mental illness, drugs, polluted politicians, world catastrophe, and global warming etc.

When Adam shifted the environment through disobedience. He moved from the place of having Gods presence enveloped in him, to shifting his world into a world of darkness. But because God had breath into Adam and brewed over him. The fragrance of God that Adam once had was now only a residue in him. Remember the scripture says after Adam ate the fruit, God walk through the garden looking for Adam.

Not that he did not know where Adam was. He knew His presence had left mankind. When God asked Adam where was he? He was asking Adam what happened to my environment? What happen to my atmosphere? Adam what did you do? God knew another system was now in operation in the environment to which He cultivated for His presence. Adam eating the fruit was the entrance to the operation of that system. Thus the fall of mankind from the presence of God.

Today, God is still looking for His environment, He wants the return of His atmosphere, His presence in His garden.

If the residue of the fragrance of God can make humanity do what is currently done. What would happened if we come into the fullness of who God is in us?

The fragrance was a marker so that man can find God. The residue which remains causes the sons of God to hunger, and thirst for more of God.

Which explains the reason why many are in search these days. Have you notice the talk of seeking God is at an all high? Can you sense there is something more? I've heard people say, "There has to be more"? "This can't be it?"

What drives many to want more is the fragrance of God and it is sleep most of the time and cannot be awaken until we come into the full knowledge of who Christ is in us. God left his fragrance to lead us back to him. He wants us to cultivate the garden in earth.

2 Corinthian 2:15 talks about the fragrance of God. It says for we are to God the pleasing aroma (fragrance) of Christ among those who are being saved and those who are perishing.
In the book of **Acts**, Paul is speaking to the perishing. In Jesus name, he commands the spirit of infirmity to exit the body. Paul understood who Christ was in him. This knowledge awakened the power of God. Paul carried the fragrance of God! The same power which Paul demonstrates is the same power which raised Jesus from the dead, now dwells within

you! The spirit that comes to quicken your mortal (natural, earthly) body is the same spirit that dwells in God.

But if the Spirit of Him who raised Jesus from the dead dwells in you, He who raised Christ from the dead will also give life to your mortal bodies through His Spirit who dwells in you. **Romans 8:11** NKJV

Ephesian 5:2 His Spirit came to make us alive in Christ Jesus.

Acts 17:28. It is in Him we are alive, that we "live and move and have our being"

1 Corinthians 6:15-17 states "Do you not know that your bodies are members of Christ?

Shall I then take the members of Christ and make them members of a harlot? Certainly not! Or do you not know that he who is joined to a harlot is one body with her? For "the two," He says, "shall become one flesh." But he who is joined to the Lord is one spirit with Him."

The whole dispensation of the Spirit, the whole economy of grace in Christ Jesus, the whole of our spiritual lives, and the whole of the health, growth, and strength of the church has been laid down, provided for, and secured in the New Covenant. - Andrew Murray

John 17:18 states "The reason the Son of God was made manifest (visible) was to undo (destroy, loosen, and dissolve) the works the devil has done." amp. You and I have access to the same given power and authority to stop death and cancel all cycles of defeat.

Mark 6:7 "And he called [unto him] the twelve, and began to send them forth by two and two; and gave them power over unclean spirits." KJV}. This power belongs to us just as it did the disciples.

1 John 3:8 states "as thou (God has sent me into the world, even so I have also sent them into the world.") You were sent from (heaven) into the world, equipped with the same glory as Jesus. **John 17: 21-23** records "that they all may be one; as thou, Father, [art] in me, and I in thee, that they also may be one in us: that the world may believe that thou hast sent me. And the **glory** which thou gavest me I have given **them**; that they may be one, even as we are one: I in them, and thou in me, that they may be made perfect in one."

I want you to understand if an infirmity or any abnormality attempts to surface within or upon you, know that it does so illegally. You are one with Christ! You have a God-given authority to rebuke the spirit in the name of Jesus and it must flee.

Psalms 91:10 states "there shall **no** evil befall thee, neither shall any **plague** come nigh thy dwelling."

Jesus took all our infirmities; this include the new sickness and diseases man creates.

The power of every infirmity was destroyed at the cross "that it might be fulfilled which was spoken by Esaias the prophet, saying, Himself took our infirmities, and bare (our) sicknesses" **Matt 8:17**. God's word states in **Isaiah 54:17** the weapon may form, but it shall not prosper.

In the context of the previous text, you can boldly declare:

Luke 10:19 "behold, he has given unto me power to tread on serpents and scorpions, and over all the power of the enemy: and nothing shall by any means hurt me" Sickness will not take my life! Depression will not take my life! Disease will not take my life! No-thing will hurt nor harm me! Command anything that gets in your way to back up and back off in the name of Jesus!

Chapter 11
6 TYPES OF PRAYERS

Ephesians 6: 18 instruct us to pray at all times with all kinds of prayer. Knowing what to pray and when to pray is very essential. These types of prayers should consist of daily decreeing and declaring. Praying these kinds of prayers prevents the enemy's plans from prevailing and stop the destruction in its way.

A. **Prayers of agreement**. Two people are touching the throne of God regarding the same thing. Jesus states that he will personally be in their midst; when this type of prayers are prayed, he hears and will answer. God wants us to see that there is extreme exzousia dunmais power in corporate, group, and united prayer. **{Genesis 11: 1-9, Matthew 18: 19-20, Exodus 17: 8-13, Psalm 133: 1-3, Acts 4:23, Hebrews 10: 24-25}**

B. **Prayers of supplication.** Is the most common form of prayer, wherein a person asks God to provide something, either for the person who is praying or for someone else on whose behalf a prayer of supplication is being made, also known as intercession **{Luke 11: 9 - 13, James 5: 17-18, 1 kings 8: 37-40, 54 – 55}**

C. **Prayers of adoration, thanksgiving and praise.** These are prayers that cause us to remember what God has done for us giving him glory, and adoration with all our heart, mind, soul and spirit telling others about his goodness, faithfulness, and love. **Psalm 100, Acts 16:16- 34, Psalm 149:4-9, 1Thessalonians 5:15-19**

D. **Prayers of faith.** This type of prayer changes things, situation and circumstances. Anything that can be seen is subject to change and can be effected by prayer of faith. It's the kind of prayer used to implement God's will into your life, earth, ministry, job, and geographical location. The Prayers of faith change things like physical ailments; employment situation, and you can have good health, and prosper in the earth.{**Mark 11:12 - 14, Mark 11: 20 - 25, Luke 7: 1 - 10, James 5: 13 - 18, Matthew 9: 18 - 26**}

E. **Prayers of warfare.** You must understand who you are as a Christian when engaging in prayer type. This is where you wage war in the heavenly realm against Satanist, demonic forces, principalities, wickedness in high places, and rulers of darkness of this world. There is a real diabolical world called the (Dark Kingdom), which you cannot see with your physical eye, yet its existence is real. This is where you get your strips as a warrior, hurls prophetic assaults to prevent the attack of the enemy.

To effectively engage in this kind of warfare, you must utilize all of your spiritual weaponry: the word of God, praying in your natural and spiritual languages, stomping, shouting, clapping, singing, praising, and walking. **Ephesians 3:6, Psalms 35, Psalms 144:1**

F. **Prayer of Intercession.** Standing in the gap and praying on behalf of someone to God. **Ezekiel 22:30** says, *"I sought for a man among them who would make a wall, and stand in the gap before Me on behalf of the land, that I should not destroy it; but I found no one."* This verse is back in the Old Testament, so He was talking to His own Jewish people when He was making these two statements. One can wonder if he is having the same problem with his people today, the born-again-Christian.{**Genesis 18: 22 -33** (Abraham) **1 Kings 18: 41 - 46** (Elijah) **2 Kings 4: 32-36 (Elisha) Acts 12: 1 – 18}** (The early church)

Note: Prayers are not given in any order of importance.

All of them should always be prayed from an offensive position. Praying before anything happens ensures this. Samson in **Judges 14:5-6** gives us an excellent picture of how we should offensively defeat the enemy, *then went Samson down, and his father and his mother, to Timnath, and came to the vineyards of Timnath: and, behold, a young lion roared against. And the Spirit of the Lord came mightily upon him, and he rent him as he would have rent a kid, and [he had] nothing in his hand: but he told not his father or his mother what he had done."* He did not allow the lion to charge at him, he ran HEAD-ON towards it, and brought it down.

God does nothing but by prayer, and everything with it.
John Wesley

Chapter 12
A GREATER MAGNITUDE

Greater works shall ye do, ye shall lay hands on the sick and they shall recover. Greater doesn't denote quantity, yet it expresses the magnitude of the work to which we shall do in his name. **Mark 16:18, Act 28:8**

The God-given authority issued to every believer is greatly enveloped with a dynamic magnitude of power. Utilizing it effectively during prayer will put a halt to, annihilate and prevent the attack of the enemy. The context implores the importance of taking our stance with dunamis power, positioned as earthly rulers and dominators, to defeat the devil in areas of our life.

Scriptures tell us that we are in Christ Jesus, and He is far above principalities, far above powers, far above wickedness, and far above rulers in high places. As He is, so are we. The enemy is not over us; he is under our feet. **Ephesians 1:21 Act 1: 4, 8** says {Do not} depart from Jerusalem but to wait for the promise of the Father...." But you shall (it's a promise, a guarantee) receive power when the Holy Spirit has come upon you; and you shall be witness to Me in Jerusalem, and in all Judea and Samaria and to the end of the earth." Every born again believer has the dunamis, exousia power to defeat the enemy,

In the **Greek** dynamis means *power, mighty work, and miracle* **Dynamis** also means exousia~ *power, authority,* exausiazo~ *have power of, exercise authority upon, bring under power.* The **Hebrew** meaning dynamis is **az.** It connotes **strong, fierce, mighty, power** oz' *strength, strong, might boldness, Hebrew for* dominion memshalan ~ *dominion, rule, government, power* mashal ~ **rule, ruler, reign, dominion, governor, ruled over, power indeed,** Greek katakyrieuo ~ **exercise dominion over, overcome be lord over** kyrieuo ~ **have dominion, exercise lordship, be lord of, lords rule,** Hebrew meaning for reign is radah ~ **rule, dominion, take prevaileth, reign** in the Greek means archo ~ **rule over, reign over** and authority in the Hebrew dynastes' ~ **potentate, of great authority.**

Do you see the miraculous power of Christ vested in you? You have been given legal authority to bring all of the works, power, influence, and affluence of Satan under your control. Put your foot down on sickness and disease; crush its head, tell it that it has come this far, but shall come no further, command it to go - it has no right to stay, you are a blood bought child of God, don't put up with it another minute. Declare that its powers are broken from touching your life, putting a cease to its works. Stop being a guinea pig; you are more than a conqueror and through Christ you can do all things! **Subdue and have dominion Ephesians 1:20-21.**

Keep your foot on the devil's neck by standing on the Word of God, and you will see tremendous results! - Jesse Duplantis

We must stand in the realm of God **Psalms 82:6** I have said that yea are gods (His legal representatives) and all of you are children of the most high. KJV, in this dimension: all power, dominion, rule, reign, authority at its maximum magnitude is in operation {**Luke 10:19**} "Behold, I give unto you power (authority) to tread on serpents and scorpions, and over all the power of the enemy: and nothing shall by any means hurt you." Within that dimension the scriptures **Isaiah 45:23** and **Romans 14:11** comes to life that says every knee must bow, and every tongue must confess His Lordship, no second guessing that every spirit including sickness and disease will confess that He is Lord.

When we prevail in this realm of prayer, we will witness the power of God growing limbs, replacing eye sockets, raising the dead, healing sickness, and all ancestral things passed down through your DNA. Remember, they have neither legal right nor choice in the matter; they have to obey the voice of God's command.

ANGELA COOPER

*Prayer does not fit us for the greater
work; prayer is the greater work.*
Oswald Chambers

Chapter 13
POWER OF THE SPOKEN WORD

Proverbs 18: 20 states: "a man shall be satisfied by the fruit of his own lips... and with the increase of his life shall he be filled." So your fulfillment in life increases when you say power packed, faith-filled words that ignite the host of heaven to respond. *{Proverbs 18:20} A man's stomach shall be satisfied from the fruit of his mouth; from the produce of his lips he shall be filled. NKJV*

Remember that our words are so powerful that God gives us a precautionary advisory written in **Proverbs 18:21** it reads, death and life are in the power of the tongue: and they that love it shall eat the fruit thereof, whatsoever you love be it life or death you are satisfied with such. Your life will be enriched with power when you decree heaven bound prayers and declarations. When I say heaven bound I mean prayers that are from that dimensional realm of rulership (saying what heaven is saying about you).

Deuteronomy 30:19 "I call heaven and earth to record this day against you, that I have set before you life and death, blessing and cursing; therefore choose life, that both thou and thy seed may live."

Heaven and earth have a prophetic mandate to act as a judge on your behalf, ruling in accordance to what you have uttered forth from your lips! It will rule in your favor or against you. Be especially cautious to what you allow to spring forth from thy mouth. You and thy seed shall be satisfied with the substance that you spew forth! If you don't want to see it tomorrow, don't speak it today. It's imperative to remember it's not what goes in the mouth that defileth a man, but that which cometh out of the mouth that defileth a man **{Matthew 15:11}**.

> *"Jesus spoke and everything he said must come to pass. That is the great plan. When we are filled only with the Holy Spirit, and we won't allow the Word of God to be detracted from by what we hear or by what we read, then comes the inspiration, then the life, then the activity, then the glory! Oh, to live it! To live in it is to be moved by it. To live in it is to be moved so that we will have God's life, God's personality in the human body."*
>
> *-Smith Wigglesworth*

At times, spirits of infirmity enter into the body through demonic portals such as bitterness, fear, resentment, anger, unwilling to forgiveness, self-rejection, broken heart, pride, rebellion, sin, self-hatred, jealousy, envy, broken spirit, doubt, and unbelief. Having a spirit of fear or torment will unlock the door to many demonic attacks. Fear comes from the root word "pho loose" meaning that which cause flight ~ act of fleeing;

There are 3 types of fear we are going to deal with.

- Fear of God (serve the Lord with fear and trembling **Psalms 2:11**)
- The fear we call upon ourselves. {*We give demonic spirits permission to exist in our life.*} (When Jesus was preparing for his final entry into Jerusalem. He called for a donkey to be brought to him, but the donkey stayed tied up until Jesus called for it. **Matthew 21:2**)
- Fear God places on a nation. A second meaning of the word fear is phobia which is persistent, irrational fear of something which is so strong that it compels us to avoid the object *ex, spiders, night, bridges, and heights, fear of people, extreme shyness, flying, enclosed spaces, and fear of success.*

Job 1 says it's the thing that Job feared the most that came upon him. Job's fear opened the door to physical, mental, emotional, psychological demonic attacks to be hurled upon him. **Psalms 34:4** tells us that when we seek the Lord, he will hear us and deliver us from all your fears. You may be at the point of losing everything you own; you may be on the bed of affiliation. Your boss may have given you a pink slip, no matter what your situation may be.

I declare to you that he has heard you, and you have no need to fear. In the word "seek" is the word "see" and when you see God, it destroys fear and you see in Him the ability to save you, and the love He has for you (Perfect love casts out all fear), {**Job 3:25, 14:22, 15:20, 33:19, Psalms 25:18, 48:6**}.

Fear of the devil is nonsense. Fear of demons is foolish. The Spirit of God anointing the Christian heart makes the soul impregnable to the powers of darkness.
- John G. Lake

Chapter 14
APPLYING THE WORD

Use the scriptures in your daily devotions. Make note cards of the scriptures to carry on your person. Study them to show yourself approved **2 Timothy 2:15.** They will empower you to overcome all the evil works of the enemy. Praying them out loud increases your faith, so then faith [cometh] by hearing, and hearing by the word of God but I say, have they not heard? Yes verily, their sound went into all the earth, and their words unto the ends of the world. **{Romans 10:17-18}.** Your words will go into all the parts of the earth awaiting the most optimum time to manifest, and will remain in the atmosphere until the end of the world.

{Matthew 18:18} Whatsoever ye bind shall be bound. Whatsoever ye loose shall be loosed. We bind and loose on earth what is bound and loosed in heaven. Whatsoever you bind render powerless is powerless. Whatsoever ye loose it is loosed whatever you say is destroy, it is destroyed.

In other word, whatever you give permission to enter into the earth realm. God gives it permission, and whatsoever you disallow God disallows. This includes sickness and disease.

Do what you can, with what you have do it now! - George Washington Carver

Faith is the assurance of things hoped for, the evidence of things not seen **{Hebrews 11:1}**.

Webster's II New College Dictionary defines faith as confident, belief in the truth values, or trustworthiness of a person, idea or thing. It also states that its beliefs not based on logical proof or material evidence. The Strong's Concordance defines faith in the Greek as ***pistis*** (G4102) meaning to be firmly persuaded.

By faith we command every mountain to be thou removed and cast into the sea, the mountain of fear, the mountain of cancer, the mountain of illness, all must go.

By faith, the centurion believed that at Jesus' word his servant would be healed. *"(And when Jesus entered into Capernaum, there came unto him a centurion, beseeching him And saying, Lord, my servant lieth at home sick of the palsy, grievously tormented. And Jesus saith unto him, I will come and heal him. The centurion answered and said, Lord, I am not worthy that thou shouldest come under my roof: but speak the word only, and my servant shall be healed. For I am a man under authority, having soldiers under me: and I say to this [man], Go, and he goeth; and to another, Come, and he cometh; and to my servant, Do this, and he doeth [it]. When Jesus heard [it], he marveled, and said to them that followed, Verily I say unto you, I have not found so great faith, no, not in Israel. And Jesus said unto the centurion, "Go thy way; and as thou hast believed, [so] be it done unto thee. And his servant was healed in the selfsame hour"* **{Matt 8:5-10, 13}**.

Hearing the word of God daily is how faith comes. God's word is quick and powerful, sharper than any two-edged sword. God's word which is the solution to today's problems moves faster than the speed of light. **Isaiah 65:24** says: "I will answer them before they even call to me. While they are still talking to me about their needs, I will go ahead and answer their prayers!" Did you catch that? Before the words fall from the creases of your lips, God has already provided the answer. It is faith without human intervention that gets the attention of heaven bringing what is unseen into the realm of the visible {*lean not unto thy own understanding, but in all thy ways acknowledge Him and He shall direct thy path* - **Proverbs 3:5, Jeremiah 33:3**}.

Faith is to believe what you do not see; the reward
of this faith is to see what you believe.
~ Saint Augustine

Chapter 15
HAVE CONFIDENCE IN GOD

And this is the confidence that we have in him, that, if we ask anything according to his will, he heareth us: and if we know that he hears us, whatsoever we ask, we know that we have the petitions that we desired of him {1John 5:14.}

Strong's G3954 says confidence is the absence of fear. Psalms 23 gives us an example of David confidently declaring Gods word, saying: "The Lord is my Shepherd and I shall not want." **(I acknowledge your Lordship there is no other God who can provide my needs).** "He maketh me to lie down in green pastures and leadeth me beside the still waters. **(He provides a place, time, and space for me to prosper).** He restoreth my soul **(he put my soul back into proper alignment with him):** he leadeth me in the paths of righteousness for his name's sake. **("He instructed me in all the right way to doing His will").**

"Yea though I walk through the valley of the Shadow of death, I will fear no evil: for thou art with me; thy rod and thy staff comfort me **(supporting me on every side)**. Thou prepare a table before me **(extending and spreading me out)** in the presence **(face)** of mine enemies thou anointest my head with oil; **(fresh revelation)** my cup runneth over **(saturating me with unspeakable joy.)** Surely goodness and mercy **(welfare, prosperity, and happiness)** shall follow **(pursue, chase,**

eagerly secure and run after) me all the days of my life: and I will dwell **(take my abode, sit down)** in the house of The Lord forever **(with** *Jehovah- the only existing one)." **Amen**

In my Summation of David's declaration:

'There is no other God who can provide a place, time, and space for my prosperity. He accurately aligns my soul, instructing me in all the right ways of doing His will. Yea though I walk through the valley of what appears to be death. I have no fear of evil because he is supporting me on every side. He extends and spreads me out in the faces of my enemies. He gives me a fresh revelation, prospering and saturating me with unspeakable joy. His welfare, prosperity, and happiness pursue, chase, eagerly secure and run after me. I will take my abode with Jehovah - the only existing one forever.'

The struggle we have today stems from a culture that has defined its reality by what is seen. Yet, Paul admonishes us to:

While we look not at the things which are seen, but at the things which are not seen: for the things which are seen *are* temporal; but the things which are not seen *are* eternal. (**2 Corinthians 4:18 – KJV**)

What is not seen has a greater eternal value than what is seen. Developing confidence in this will take a shift in our mindset. There has to be a renewing of our minds to the reality that God is, and He can be trusted.

I have heard Christian voice their concerns and worries when the topic of faith comes up. If God is a great protector, why are

His people meeting in accidents, some even tragic? Why can they be held up and robbed at gunpoint? Why are their homes, and even church, broken into and valuable items are stolen? How can I have confidence in God that I am protected when I see others who are not? This kind of thinking also spill over in God being our provider. If God provides and supplies all my needs, then why am I still in lack?

The mysteries of the Kingdom of God sometimes provokes more questions than answers. We must acknowledge that the promises of God come with conditions. The only thing constant and unconditional that He extends to us is His love. When we trust God, and put our confidence in Him, we will not be ashamed.

Fear not; for thou shalt not be ashamed: neither be thou confounded; for thou shalt not be put to shame: for thou shalt forget the shame of thy youth, and shalt not remember the reproach of thy widowhood any more. (**Isaiah 54:4 – KJV**)

It is not confidence to test God. We pray sometimes, and stand aside to see if God will do something. That is confidence. Confidence is knowing without the shadow of a doubt that God will do exactly what He says He will do. It is this kind of confidence that produces faith, and opens the door to peace that surpasses all understanding, regardless of what is happening around us.

You may be facing a storm in your life right now. You may have more questions than answers. Put your confidence in God, and rest in His promises.

Then Jesus said, "Come to me, all of you who are weary and carry heavy burdens, and I will give you rest. Take my yoke upon you. Let me teach you, because I am humble and gentle at heart, and you will find rest for your souls. (**St. Matthew 11:28-29 – NLT**)

People who ask confidently get more than
those who are hesitant and uncertain.
When you've figured out what you want to ask for,
do it with certainty, boldness and confidence.
-Jack Canfield

Chapter 16
PRAY IN THE SPIRIT

Ephesians 6:18 "Keep on praying in the spirit at all times with all kinds of prayer." Praying in the spirit builds you up. To build means to construct by putting parts or material together over a period of time: In many respects the foundation is the most important element of any building, be it a house or a high-rise. Simply put, the foundation is what everything rests on. So getting the foundation right will go a long way toward having a sound and stable building for many years. Praying in the spirit is as laying the foundation to a house. Your spiritual house is equally important. Over time praying in the spirit brings the secrets of God's Spirit into your spirit. Praying builds up your own spiritual strength. It makes you strong in the Lord. Releases you into a higher dimension of worship. Your speaking in tongues aide in the ability for others to hear from God. **Jude 1:20-21** states But ye, beloved, building up yourselves on your most holy faith, praying in the Holy Ghost, Keep yourselves in the love of God, looking for the mercy of our Lord Jesus Christ unto eternal life. Every mature believer along with praying in your natural language should pray daily in the language of the kingdom of heaven (tongues). It is direct communication with the Father. It allows access for the Holy Spirit's entry into the earth.

Each time, before you intercede, be quiet first, and worship God in His glory. Think of what He can do, and how He delights to hear the prayers of His redeemed people. Think of your place and privilege in Christ, and expect great things! - Andrew Murray

Spend time in worship, praise, and thanksgiving.

There are many advantages that one will obtain when praising and worshipping the Father.

1. It causes your enemies to turn on themselves. (The trap that the enemy has set up for my fall he will fall in it **Psalms 35:8**. (**2 Chronicles 20:22**) states: "And when they began to sing and praise God, the Lord set ambushes against the men of Ammon and Moab and Mount Seir who were invading Judah, and they were defeated." The Ammonites and Moabites rose up against the men from Mount Seir to destroy and annihilate them. After they had finished slaughtering the men from Seir, they helped to destroy one another.
2. It brings provision and removes sickness away from you. **Exodus 23:25** "And ye shall serve the Lord your God, and he shall bless thy bread and thy water and I will take sickness away from the midst of thee."
3. It gives God permission to counsel you during the times of joy and when thou art heavy. (**Isaiah 61:3**.) "I will bless the Lord who has given me counsel, my reigns also instruct me in the night season" (**Psalms 16:7**).
4. It brings your life into stability "(I standeth in an even place in the congregation I will bless the Lord.)" (**Psalms 26:12**).

5. It brings everything in your life into divine alignment and godly order. ("A double minded man is unstable in all his ways, but in the counsel of the Lord there is safety" **James 1:8**).

6. It Gives access to an elaborate benefit package, filled with peace, joy, prosperity, success, wealth, extravagance, royalty, love, intimacy, ecstasy, greatness, and many blessings of the Lord. "I will bless the Lord O' my soul and all that is within me. Bless the Lord O' my soul and forget not all his benefits who forgiveth all thine iniquities who healeth all thy disease **(Psalms 103:2-3).**

7. It reveals how deeply the Father loves us, bringing to remembrance the power of the crucifixion, the forgiveness and removal of sins.

8. It causes your healing to spring forth **(Isaiah 58: 8).**

9. It reminds us how good God is and gives us access to the safety that's found only in Him *(He who dwells in the secret place shall abide under the shadow of the almighty Psalms 91:1).*

10. It causes the Father's attention to be turned toward you *(you have the mind of Christ) you are on his mind* 1 Co.2:16. ("For I know the thoughts that I think toward you, saith the Lord, thoughts of peace, and not of evil, to give you an expected end." **Jeremiah 29:11**)

Worship, in a very real sense of the word, opens a doorway to the power of His presence, confounding dark powers and overthrowing sin's destructive operations. - Jack Hayford

Chapter 17
CONFESS YOUR SINS

Come to God with a humble heart. Examine yourself daily, to see if you need to confess, repent, release or forgive someone, be specific with Him not. He already knows what you did. He wants you to acknowledge that you have sinned, and He wants you to know that He already forgives.

As He forgives us, we should also forgive others.

(James 5: 16) Confess your faults one to another, and pray one for another, that ye may be healed. The effectual fervent prayer of a righteous man availeth much. **KJV**

> *Forgiving does not erase the bitter past. A healed*
> *memory is not a deleted memory. Instead,*
> *forgiving what we cannot forget creates a new*
> *way to remember. We change the memory*
> *of our past into a hope for our future.*
> *-- Lewis B. Smedes*

Make certain to have daily communion with God

Make certain not to take Gods communion lightly **1 Corinthians 11: 29-30**! Remember: partaking in Communion is a holy time of worship when we corporately come together as one body to remember and celebrate what Christ did for us. In observing Communion, we remember Christ and all that He has done for us in his life, death and resurrection. And when he had given thanks, he broke it and said, "This is my body, which is for you; do this in remembrance of me" **{1 Corinthians 11:24}**.

1 Corinthians 11:25-27, in the same manner he took the cup.

When observing Communion, we take the time to examine ourselves: "A man ought to examine himself before he eats of the bread and drinks of the cup" **{1 Corinthians 11:28}**. In observing Communion, we are proclaiming His death until He comes. It is, then, a statement of faith: "For whenever you eat this bread and drink this cup, you proclaim the Lord's death until he comes" **{1 Corinthians 11:26}**. When we observe Communion, we show our participation in the body of Christ. His life becomes our life, and we become members of each other:

"Is not the cup of thanksgiving for which we give thanks a participation in the blood of Christ? And is not the bread that we break a participation in the body of Christ? Because there is one loaf, we, who are many, are one body, for we all partake of the one loaf." **{1 Corinthians 10:16-17, Matthew 26:26-27, Mar. 14:23, Luke 22:17, Matthew 10:18, 38-39, 52, John 6:35, 53, Luke 5:31}**

When we break the bread it is a symbol of the brokenness of the body of Christ. But the good thing about it is that it is a brokenness that can be reconstituted. We would have a problem if Jesus had broken the bread and thrown it away. But He broke it and gave to His disciples to eat which mean that when the bread is eaten it becomes whole because it provides life for the person who eats it. It becomes a part of the body of the people who eat it as a reconnection to the life that is Christ. Communion is powerful, it symbolizes that there is no brokenness that cannot be fixed.

Loss of communion is the explanation of most of our failure in spiritual fruit bearing. - Donald Gee

Just as priests applied the blood in the old covenant, we as priests in the new covenant are to use the blood of Jesus. *This is the blood of the testament which God hath **enjoined** unto you.* (**Hebrews 9:20**) The word enjoined means to be given charge of. In the old covenant, the priest applied the blood of animals by sprinkling. In the new covenant, we receive the blood by faith and sprinkle the blood with our words. *For with the heart one believes unto righteousness, and with the mouth confession is made unto salvation.* (**Romans 10:10**) You apply the blood of Jesus to yourself when you say, "the blood of Jesus which He shed on the cross was for me, and it makes me free from sin and all unrighteousness." Overcoming is a continual process in this life.

I've heard many pray as such "I plead the blood of Jesus over this situation or that circumstance." We are never to plead for the blood of Jesus. To plea means to beg, we are not beggars, we are sons, it is our covenantal right to having liberal access according to the word of God, to apply it as necessary. Whatever we apply the blood of Jesus to Satan cannot touch. Whatever we apply the blood to becomes redeemed by Christ, it becomes His. Whatever we apply the blood to is made Holy.

When the blood is applied so also is God's grace and the anointing of Holy Spirit applied. When we apply the body and blood of Jesus. We speak into our bones and marrow at the genetic level. We say "be transformed into the image of Jesus; be genetically purified and transformed from one degree of glory to another. Be ye transformed, transfigured and radiate glory. Whenever we eat and drink, we can take it as the body and blood of Jesus. With the words that are spirit and life. Speaking to our marrow; we apply the DNA of God to transform your DNA into the eternal image of God that is your destiny. Let's do this regularly, every day if possible, because there is awesome power in it.

We overcome by the blood of the Lamb, Jesus Christ, and the word of our testimony. Through the blood of Jesus, and our witness to it, we overcome and have the power to give our life entirely for the One who gave His life for us. We apply the blood by the word of our testimony. In the old covenant, they applied the blood by sprinkling, (Hebrew 9:19). In the new covenant we apply the blood by our words.

Every Christian's testimony has the same beginning; it began on the cross of Jesus Christ. The shed blood of Jesus Christ is the most important part of any testimony. Without the blood, we have no testimony. On the cross is where our testimony began, on the cross is where we were transformed, and on the cross is where we were crucified with Jesus. I have been crucified with Christ; it is no longer I who live, but Christ lives in me; and the life which I now live in the flesh I live by faith in the Son of God, who loved me and gave Himself for me. (**Galatians 2:20**)

You can apply the blood of Jesus to your body to receive healing, *{Isaiah 53:5}.* You can apply the blood of Jesus to your mind, to receive a sound mind. You can apply the blood of Jesus to your home, (***Exodus 12:13***). You can apply the blood of Jesus to your children, (***Job 1:5).*** You can apply the blood of Jesus to anyone and anything that you have authority over or influence upon. It is your right as God's child.

When there is a lack of anointing, examine yourself in regard to the Blood. The Blood is the legal basis of authority; the Holy Spirit does the actual empowering. - David Alsobrook

Chapter 18
RELEASE HIS ANGELS

<u>Psalms 91:11</u> tell us that God gives His angels charge over thee, to keep thee in all thy ways, angels are to be in charge over our lives. Each person has a guardian angel. Believers who fear God have a troop of angels encamped about them. Ps 103:20 states "Bless the Lord ye his angel that excel in strength that do his commandments harkening unto the voice of his word."

They are to assist us in ministry, protect, guard, watch, instruct, defend, comfort, speak, guide and bring us messages from God.

"See, I am sending an angel ahead of you to guard you along the way and to bring you to the place I have prepared. Pay attention to him and listen to what he says. Do not rebel against him; he will not forgive your rebellion, since my name is in him. If you listen carefully to what he says and do all that I say, I will be an enemy to your enemies and will oppose those who oppose you. My angel will go ahead of you and bring you into the land of the Amorites, Hittites, Perizzites, Canaanites, Hivites and Jebusites, and I will wipe them out. Do not worship them or follow their practices. You must demolish them and break their sacred stones to pieces. Worship the Lord your God, and I will take away sickness from among you, and none will miscarry or be barren in your land. I will give you a full life span" {<u>Exodus 23: 20-25</u>}.

Blessed assurance, Jesus is mine oh what a foretaste of glory divine. Heir of salvation, purchased of God, born of his spirit, washed in his blood. Perfect submission, perfect delight vision of rapture now burst on my sight. Angels descending bring from above echoes of mercy, whispers of love.
Fanny J. Crosby.

Jeremiah 33:22 states "The host of heaven cannot be counted and the sand of the sea cannot be measured." There are an unfathomable number of angels called a googolplex. Scripture put it to us this way in **Psalms 68:17** "The chariots of God are tens of thousands and thousands of thousand; the Lord has come from Sinai into his sanctuary" Angels have shapes, forms and colors, races, and nations, with wings and four faces **Psalms 104:4** states who maketh his angels spirit his minister a flaming of fire. KJV They are soldiers, messengers, and ministering angels. "Praise the Lord, you his angels you mighty ones, who do his bidding who obey his word" {*Psalms 103: 20*}.

Let us reason for a little bit. Angels are Messengers, and Warriors who fight and do battle on behalf of the Lord. They carry out His commandments, and serve Him in absolute obedience and submission. What is the purpose of angels and heavenly host in heaven, where God dwells? Does heaven need an angelic army? Do they need messengers to carry the Word of the Lord around to their occupants? I submit that the purpose of angels is intricately tied to the earth, and humanity.

Jacob once found himself in a particular place, and he had a dream:

And he dreamed, and behold a ladder set up on the earth, and the top of it reached to heaven: and behold the angels of God ascending and descending on it. (**Genesis 28:12 – KJV**)

This is the reality of the spiritual world, a daily occurrence.

And he dreamed, and behold a ladder set up on the earth, and the top of it reached to heaven: and behold the angels of God ascending and descending on it. (**St. John 1:51 – KJV**)

This is your daily reality as a son of God. I have heard several ministers who say they see in the spirit claim that a lot of angels operating in Christians life is bored, and underutilized. Angels are moved into action by the Word of God, by what we speak. Our words either empower the evils spirits around us, or they empower the angels. Why do you think we are cautioned to be mindful of what we say? We no longer live in an age where our words fall to the ground. You will eat the fruits of what you speak.

Angels are assigned to work alongside us to fulfill our divine destiny. We have a responsibility to learn all we can about them, so we can align ourselves with them, and partner with them to fulfill God's call on our lives. They have shielded us more times than you know.

God's angels often protect his servants from potential enemies- Billy Graham

Chapter 19
PRAY IN THIS MANNER

According to **Matthew 6:9,** when Jesus was asked by the disciples on how to pray, He instructed the disciples to pray in the following manner: "Our father which art in heaven, hallowed be thy name, thy kingdom come, thy will be done in earth as it is in heaven, give us this day our daily bread, and forgive us our debts as we forgive our debtor, and lead us not into temptation but delivers us from evil, for thine is the Kingdom and the power and the glory forever amen." For the next few minutes, we are going to dissect this passage of scripture into 5 sections.

1. "Our father which art in heaven, hallowed be thy name." The first and most relevant portion of the text reveals to us the right kind of relationship we're to have with God. For us to call him father, we first must come into covenant relationship with him. We do this by accepting Jesus Christ as our lord (ruler, master) and savior thus bringing us into position to be called the sons of God. Secondly, it places us in a position of worship, declaring His name sacred, acknowledging Him as our father, (daddy) provider, shelter, strength, etc. Thirdly, it identifies His realm of dominion through man in the earth.

2. "Thy kingdom come, thy will de done in earth as it is in heaven." Our earthly mandate here in the earth is to do the will of the Father, not our own. We must daily seek to *"see"* His kingdom, which is an everlasting kingdom. The Greek defines kingdom as **basileia**- it is the rule, reign, dominion, and power of God. The word kingdom is a compound word. Firstly, King in the Hebrew is **mamlakah**- kingdom, royal, reigns. The Greek word is **Basileia,** kingdom of heaven, kingdom of God and reign.

The second half of the word is *dom.* The Hebrew word is **mashal**- rule, ruler, reign, dominion, governor, ruled over, power. Indeed, the second Hebrew word is **rada**- rule, dominion, take, prevaileth, reign, ruler.

The Greek gives us several words: katayrieuo – exercise, dominion over, overcome, be lord, of lord, exercise lordship over. **Kratos**-power, dominion, strength, might. **Kyrieuo**- have dominion, exercise lordship over, be lord of lords. **Kyriotes**- means dominion, government.

We can establish from the meanings that God desires for His government to have rulership and dominion here on the earth (in you and me). We are to manifest His will. It requires seeking the Father daily, to know what He's already established in heaven, In order to establish it through prayer in the earth. It is here that we will begin our decrees, releasing the governor (Holy Spirit) of heaven into the earth. His kingdom is within you and is worked through you, and it wants to come out of you {**Matthews 6: 33**, **Revelations 11:15, Daniel 4:3, 4:34, 7:14**}.

3. "Give us this day our daily bread." One tactic of the enemy is to steal, kill and destroy. The devil desires to steal our day and all of its sustaining resources. God asked Job if he'd commanded his morning since the day began and caused the dawn to know its place **(Job 38:12)**. One definition of the word command is *required obedience.* It is here that we can require our day to cooperate, and obey with the plan of God for our life. Secondly, ask the Father for life's daily provisions; He will withhold no good thing from you {**Psalms 84:11**}. Matt 6:31 illustrates to us how much he cares for the birds of the air. What more will he care for you being his child? "Whatever it is that ye ask for when ye pray believe that ye shall receive it" {**1 John14:15**}.

4. "Forgive us our debts as we forgive our debtors and lead us not into temptation." Here we can see the importance of having a clean and pure heart before the Lord. "Who may ascend into the hill of the Lord? Who may stand in his holy place? He who has clean hands and a pure heart, who does not lift up his soul to an idol or swear by what is false" {**Psalms 24: 3-4**}. As you forgive others who are indebted towards you, so does the Heavenly Father forgives you. Secondly, we can see him as a Good Shepherd, never leading us into a place where we are tempted by worldly enticements {**James 1:13**}.

5. "For thine is the kingdom and the power and the glory forever amen." Jesus brings us back into our intimate place of worship. Spending time telling Him that He is all powerful, that He reigns, that He rules, giving Him glory forever, causes you to have unlimited access to His elaborate kingdom.

Chapter 20
PREPARE FOR BATTLE

The prayers you are about to embark upon was constructed in a way for you to:

- Receive a paradigm shift in the way you pray and believe in God's word.
- Build your faith.
- Receive immediate results.
- Effectively war in the heavenlies for you and your loved ones.
- Pray and see miracles.
- Defeat the enemy at his own game.
- Release the Angels of the Lord to fight for you.
- Be equipped and strengthened to command hell to back up.

Praying them aloud will cause the atmosphere around you to be impregnated with power. **Romans 10:17** states that "Faith cometh by hearing and hearing by the word of God." The more you listen to the word of God spoken, the more your faith increase, **Hebrews 11:1** states that "now faith is the substance of things hoped for, the evidence of things not seen." You don't have to wait until you feel change nor see it; now faith is, you will have whatsoever you say when you pray, at the moment you speak it shall be done for you. **Job 22:28** says that when a king decrees a thing it shall be done for him and the light shall shine upon thy ways.

Chapter 21
ACTIVATION/DECLARATION

I like the model that Jesus established with His disciples. He chose them, then poured into them, and then He sent them out in His authority and power.

I have given you authority to trample on snakes and scorpions and to overcome all the power of the enemy; nothing will harm you. (St. Luke 10:19)

You have been chosen when you took up this book. You have been taught throughout the pages, and now you will be activated to go and make good what you know. Before you pray the prayer of faith, you must be activated.

And without faith it is impossible to please God, because anyone who comes to him must believe that he exists and that he rewards those who earnestly seek him. (Hebrews 11:6)

Declare: "*I have enough faith to please God. I believe that He exists, and He will reward me for earnestly seeking Him.*"

When you approach God in prayer, do so in boldness. Recognize that in His eyes you are a son or a daughter, and He loves you. He is more than willing to hear what you have to say, and to respond favorably as any loving father would. Don't seek to determine any progress made by your emotions, or by what you see. Faith operates at a much higher level than our senses. It is not a position of standing aside to see if God will or has done anything, but knowing that He will.

And the prayer offered in faith will make the sick person well; the Lord will raise them up. If they have sinned, they will be forgiven. (James 5:15 – NIV)

As you pray, guard your heart and your mind and refuse any doubt, questions or concerns access to your thoughts. Hold fast to the confession of the Word of God, even amidst glaring inconsistencies.

Declare: *"I will pray the prayer of faith that will make me well, because the Lord will raise me up. If I have sinned, He will forgive me."*

James cautions us about having a double mind when we approach God:

But when you ask, you must believe and not doubt, because the one who doubts is like a wave of the sea, blown and tossed by the wind. That person should not expect to receive anything from the Lord. Such a person is double-minded and unstable in all they do. (James 1:6-7 – NIV)

To experience healing, faith is a necessary by-product of receiving from the Lord. We must be confident, bold and specific. All that God could do to secure our healing, and make it possible to walk in divine health, has already been done long before we even got here. Jesus was crucified before the foundations of the earth, so the debt for sickness was already paid. Our challenge is to appropriate in our own lives what has already been done.

But he was pierced for our transgressions, he was crushed for our iniquities; the punishment that brought us peace was on him, and by his wounds we are healed. (Isaiah 53:5 – NIV)

"He himself bore our sins" in his body on the cross, so that we might die to sins and live for righteousness; "by his wounds you have been healed." (1 Peter 2:24 – NIV)

Declare: *"My sins have been paid for. The debt for any and all sicknesses, infirmities and disease has been met. Therefore, infirmity, sickness and disease is illegal to operate in my body. It has no grounds or place in my life on the merit of the finished work on the cross. Jesus has already paid the wages for my sin, so I don't have to."*

There is no one in this world who can exercise faith in Jesus, without doubting, and not see any results. When you pray, believe.

We have entered what is known as the kingdom age, where divine health is now being released to the body of Christ. Miracles of healing and restoration are no longer an isolated instance centered around one radical Christian who have broken free from the status quo, to pursue the God of the Bible who heals, even what man would label as incurable.

Several years ago, there was a man named Smith Wigglesworth who spent a considerable amount of time in prayer, and study of the Word. He believed in the Word of God, and it was established in his heart as the only truth. One of his famous, and favorite quotes was, "Only Believe." That is all you need to do Beloved, 'Only Believe.'

Please lay your hands on your head, as you read the following prayer and as an act of faith:

Father, I thank you for everyone who is reading this book. I pray for a fresh impartation and activation now of the gift of Your Spirit to heal, deliver and set free. Whoever the Son sets free, is truly free indeed. May you stir up and release what You have already placed inside them, as they prepare to contend for the faith You expect every believer to have. We come against any hindering spirits that would resist in the heavenlies the release of Your power, and the answer to our prayers. We come against the spirit of doubt and fear that will attempt to dilute our faith, and render it ineffective. We come against the voice of the stranger who would insight rebellion, and cast doubt on the validity of Your promises. We pray for and receive a renewed mind that will accept, and not reject the truth. Father, you value Your Word above Your Name, so may everyone who completes this book receive that which they are seeking You for, in Jesus Name.

Declare: *"Your Word says, "Whatever I ask for in prayer, believe that I have received it, and it will be mine." You also said, "You will do what I ask for in Your Name, so that the Father will be glorified in the Son." Lord, may Your Name be glorified today as I stand on Your Word. I declare that I will have what I say. I declare that You have spoken the truth God, and every other voice is lying. I will stand on Your truth, believing that You will honor the integrity of Your Word. What You have spoken is already established."*

Chapter 22
PRAY ALOUD

Our Father, and our God, who art in heaven hallowed be thy name, thy kingdom come, thy will be done on earth as it is in Heaven. As I seek you, I ask you to download your will during this strategic prayer time. I ascend into the mountain of the Lord to hear what the king has to say to me. I pray your will in the earth for my life.

Let the words of my mouth and the meditation of my heart be acceptable in thy sight, oh Lord my God **Psalms 19:14**. I confess and repent of my sin, and release everyone who has hurt me, undermined me, stabbed me in the back, spoken against me, or lied to me. Create in me a clean heart and renew a right spirit within me {**Psalms 51:10**}.

I release the fire of the Lord from my mouth to destroy the tactics of the enemy. Your word says that the diligent shall bear rule. I am diligent, so therefore, I rule over every evil work of the enemy plaguing my life.

It is you who giveth life and that more abundantly. I thank and praise thee for all spiritual blessing in heavenly places. The atmosphere around me changes now; as I praise your name. As I praise You oh God, a two-edged sword is released into my hands to destroy and annihilate the plans of the enemy!

Right now in Jesus' name, I decree and declare: The heavens are opening. I open portals and channels in the realms of the spirit. I decree and declare I have successful travel with angelic undergirding as I go into new levels, new realms, and new dimensions. I have clear access now.

My Father and healer, as I announce your irrevocable word into the atmosphere, your angels respond, releasing spiritual substance, power, dominion, and authority.

Father, your word says "the heavens are the Lord's heavens, but the earth He has given to the children of men" {**Psalms 115:16**}.

My will now is to do the will of Him that sent me. Like Jesus, I do what I see my Father in heaven doing, I say what I am hearing my Father saying in heaven.

I decree that my mind and body function according to the Creator's original plan and purposes for it. I decree and declare that the weapons of my warfare are not carnal, but mighty through God {**Ephesians 6: 13-18**}. I place the whole armor of the Lord upon myself {**Ephesians 6:11**}.

Chapter 23
HEALING FOR THE MIND

The gods of this age have blinded the minds of unbelievers, so that they cannot see the light of the gospel of Christ, who is the image of God **2 Corinthians 4:4**.

I pull down and cast out ~ the strongholds of doubt, fear, unbelief, rejection, hatred, anger, lust, harlotry, perverseness, self-accusation, timidity, and selfishness in the name of Jesus.

I loose ~ my mind from bondage, chains, cords, snares, fetters, and restore the fragmented soul. I will not speak contrary against what you are saying concerning me in the heavens.

I bind my mind to the mind of Christ.

I loose ~ every perverse spirit now in the name of Jesus. Now Father, I thank you for not only do I have your mind so that I can think your thoughts. I'm also on your mind, and I have understood that your attention and your thoughts towards me are for good and not for evil. Therefore, I will think only of things that are true, pure, and of a good report {**Philippians 4:8-9**}.

For **Psalms 139:13-18** states "For you did form my inward parts; you did knit me together in my mother's womb.

I will confess and praise You for You are fearful and wonderful and for the awful wonder of my birth! Wonderful are Your works, and that my inner self know right well.

My frame was not hidden from you when I was being formed in secret and intricately and curiously wrought (as if embroidered with various colors) in the depths of the earth (a region of darkness and mystery).

Your eyes saw my unformed substance, and in Your book all the days (of my life) were written before they took shape, when yet there was none of them. How precious and weighty also are your thoughts to me, O God!

How vast is the sum of them! If I could count them, they would be more in number than the sand when I awoke, (could I count to the end) I would still be with You."

Now unto the only wise God, to him who is able to do exceedingly abundantly above all that I can imagine ask or think according to the power that worketh in me {**Ephesians 3:20**}.

For though I live in this world, I do not wage war as the world does; the weapons I fight with are not the weapons of this world. On the contrary, they have divine power to demolish strongholds.

I demolish ~ arguments and every pretension that set itself against the knowledge of God, and I take captive every thought to make it obedience to Christ {**2 Corithians 10: 3-5**}.

I command the spirits of schizophrenia, bipolar disease, nervousness, anxiety, doublemindedness, hyperactivity, attention deficit disorder, feelings of pity, low self-esteem, low self-image, self-mutilation, mental retardation, all learning disabilities, dyslexia, imaginary friends, day dreaming, wrongful thoughts, suicidal thoughts, depression, oppressions, rebellion, insecurity, inferiority, all compulsive behaviors, fantasy, talkativeness, tension, paranoia, suspicion, hopelessness, discouragement, despair, to come out now in the name of Jesus, you have no authority over me and return to the pits of hell.

I speak to the left brain and the right brain divine alignment.

I speak to the frontal lobe which gives balance; line up in the name of Jesus!

I speak balance to the Hypothalamus and Thalamus gland.

I speak to the limbic system which controls mood and emotions: regulate, you will not misfire.

I speak to the brain matter and command you to control unconscious functions.

I lay my hands on my head and command every demonic spirit to come out! Come out of the left brain, come out of the right brain, and come out of the all four lobes, I send you back to the sender.

I decree and declare ~ mass deliverance.

Father, have your way now.

I speak ~ that the blood flows freely and in the name of Jesus, I'm free from aneurysms, strokes, comas, blood clots, tumors, hemorrhage in the brain, etc.

I cancel ~ diabolical soul ties and relationships that are designed to hinder and frustrate my life.

I rebuke ~ the spirits of Jezebel and Belial that come to take my self-worth.

I am fearfully and wonderfully made in your image and after your likeness. I am the apple of your eye and I am very good. In replace of a spirit of heaviness, according to **Isaiah 61:3** I loose a spirit of praises, honor, respect, celebration, esteem, reverence and extol in my life in Jesus' name.

I decree and declare that no weapon formed against my life, health, bones, kidney, liver, blood, cells, lymphatic system, hypothalamic system, lungs, throat, eyes, organs, head, marrow, breast, spleen, spine, pancreas, ears, mouth, tongue, sinuses, legs and toes shall prosper.

I speak to every prevailing principality and powers that have established themselves as spiritual gatekeepers and doorkeepers to these spiritual borders: I break your powers and render you powerless. I command you to back up and back off now in the name of Jesus!

I arrest every evil spirit, and every evil principality that comes to bring sickness, that comes to bring disease, that comes to bring plagues, and that comes to bring rare illness.

I command ~ every principality and power to lift up your head and be ye lifted up yea everlasting doors that the King of glory may come in. "Who is the King of Glory the Lord strong and mighty! The Lord mighty in battle mighty to save, mighty to deliver"! {**Psalm 24:9**} I establish Jesus as the gatekeeper and door- keeper to these spiritual borders!

I decree that no bacteria, germ, and infection will touch my body, in the name of Jesus. I decree that no weapon formed against my fingers, hands, wrists, feet, teeth, gums, back, shoulders, eyelashes, hair, scalp, and arteries shall prosper and every tongue that rises up against me I shall condemn {**Isaiah 54:17**}.

I decree ~ every sickness, disease, physical and emotional illness to be inhabitable now in Jesus, according to {**Isaiah 53:5**}.

Chapter 24
HEALING FOR INTERNAL ORGAN

I decree and declare ~ that no evil shall befall thee nor plague shall come nigh my dwelling {**Psalms 91:10**}! I decree healing and strength to my life, health, bones, kidneys, hands, feet, teeth, gums, strength, arteries, veins, blood vessels, liver, blood, cells, lymphatic system, hypothalamic system, lungs, throat, eyes, organs, head, marrow, breast, spleen, spine, pancreas, ears, mouth, tongue, sinuses, legs, toes, fingers, back, wrists, shoulders, all function according to the Creator's design.

I decree ~ that I'm prosperous and walk in good health even as my soul prospers.

Healing for Physical Deterioration

I decree and declare ~ according to **Psalms 27:2** that I'm free from all flesh-eating disease including cancer, measles, necrotizing fasciitis, Alzheimer's, amyotrophic lateral sclerosis, bulimia, anorexia nervosa, appendicitis, motor neuron disease, acne, Reye's syndrome, psoriasis, scarlet fever, addiction, AIDS, alcoholism, allergies, silicosis. I decree in the name of Jesus that the fire of God burns every tumor and evil, malignant growth {**Psalms 97:5**}.

I decree ~ that I will only hear good reports making my bones fat and making my flesh healthy. My bones will never be broken {**Proverbs. 15:30**, **Proverbs. 4:22**, **Psalms 34:20**}.

I decree and declare that I'm free from any and all ancestral curses, sickness or disease.

I decree ~ that the anointing on my life repels gout, Lyme disease, mad cow disease, meningitis, rheumatoid arthritis, multiple sclerosis, gout, optic neuritis, myocarditis, diverticulitis, thyroiditis, leukemia, Graves disease, Crohn's disease, fibromyalgia, Huntington's, Tay-Sachs, fragile x syndrome, Down's syndrome, kuru, all forms of sickle cell disease, all of anemia, Parkinson's, deformity, dementia, lethargy and all forms of lupus from touching my life {**Isaiah 10:27**}.

I command that the spirit of pain to leave my body and I will live a pain-free life in the name of Jesus.

Healing for 12 Major Systems

I decree and declare ~ that I have divine health and maintain proper protocol in all of the following systems: cardiovascular system, endocrine system, pulmonary system, psychological system, neurological system, renal system, reproductive system, dermatological system, immune system, musculoskeletal system, and hematological system.

I decree and declare ~ that I'm free from heart attack, stroke, renal failure, angina, coronary artery disease, cerebral vascular disease, all major organs are free from plaque and cholesterol and chronic chest pain

{**Psalms. 118: 17**}. I shall live and not die and declare your works! I decree that I'm free from all curses of premature death, comas, and destructive tactics of the enemy.

Healing from STD

In **Psalms 107:20** You sent Your word and healed every disease. I decree and declare that I'm free from herpes complex 1 and 2, syphilis, gonorrhea, genital warts, lymphogranuloma, yeast infection, bacterial vaginosis, trichomoniasis, chancroids, scabies, hepatitis, vaginitis, granuloma, Chlamydia, UTI, molluscum, and pubic lice. I command ~ them to come out {**John 1: 1-3, 14-16**}! I ask that you give me this day as I shake evil out of it. Give me my daily provisions, everything which pertains to life and godliness.

Thank you for sending Your word to heal all my disease. Jehovah Rohpe, you are the Lord, my healer!

Chapter 25
PRAYER TO RELEASE ANGELS

Now Father I ask for Godly warring angels to bind evil spirits with chains and take them to dry places, Abyss or Tartarus.

I loose ~ angels to bruise, crush and flatten the heads of the serpentine spirits and to snip off the tails of the scorpion spirits.

I release ~ Michael the warring angel and the archangel and all angelic hosts to war against those that are warring against me (**Daniel 10**). I call for the Angel of the Lord to fight for me.

~I ask God to send guardian angels, warrior angels, and twelve legions of angels as reinforcement for spiritual and physical warfare on my behalf.

I ask ~for warrior angels to protect me and fight for me.

I ask ~the angels to remove the ropes, shackles, chains, bond and bands from around me (**Psalms 34:7**; **Psalms 91:11-13 Hebrews 1:14**).

Lord, send angels ahead of me to prepare the way, let angels go with me everywhere I go. Let the angels cremate the demons that would attempt to harm me. Lord, send your anger, wrath, indignation and trouble to every evil spirit who comes to destroy me.

I send ~armies of warring angels to attack. I will utilize every scripture that has been given to me by God the Father, that wars against the demonic forces.

May the angel of the Lord be released to persecute and chase the enemy. {**Psalms 35:6**} You, O Lord, will send your angels and rid the heavens of any satanic contention. That Angels of the Lord most high smite every demon that comes to destroy my life {**Isaiah 37:36**}.

"Now unto him that able to do exceedingly abundantly above all that I can imagine ask or think according to the power that worketh in me {**Ephesians 6**}.

Chapter 26
PRAYERS TO BIND AND TO LOSE

I use the power you have given me, God, to bind and subdue Satan's Empire. As I enter spiritual warfare and assault the kingdom of darkness, I bind the forces of evil and destroy the kingdom of evil.

I bind ~ principalities, power, rulers of the darkness of this world and spiritual wickedness in high places.

Lord lead me not into temptation but deliver me from evil and the evil one. Hide me in the safety of your counsel.

I bind ~ demonic spirits and cast them out. I lose godly spirits to do their work.

I bind ~ forces of Satan and free forces of God where I have power and authority. I bind the kingdom of evil, darkness.

I bind ~ demonic efforts to kill, steal and destroy. I loose the Holy Spirit, the seven-fold spirit of God, a price that Jesus Christ paid, the Love of God, Holy Spirit, Word of God, Blood of Jesus Christ, and Cross of Jesus Christ and power of God to lose me and do a mighty battle on earth against the Kingdom of Evil.

I bind and order ~ demons to return to hell, escorted by angels to destroy the seats of witchcraft. Jesus, you are my deliverer, so therefore, deliver me with your fire and I am delivered and made free.

I decree and declare ~ that I'm free from the curses sent through witchcraft, voodoo, black magic, white magic, enchantment, tealeaf reading, sorcery and incantations **Psalms 18:13**

I command ~ the spirits of fear and anxiety which come to raise my heart and blood pressure, to come out now in Jesus' name.

I command ~ the spirits of bitterness, resentment and unforgiveness, which open the door to cancer, to come out of my life now {**Job 21:25, Job 10: 1, 9:18**}.

I bind ~ the spirits of rejection, self-hatred, guilt, rooted in diabetes, rheumatoid arthritis sinus, allergies and multiple sclerosis; paralysis. I loose love, joy, righteousness and peace in the Holy Spirit.

I decree and declare ~ as Jesus states in {**St. John 10:18**} "No man takes my life I lay it down," I decree and declare in the name of Jesus I will nor die, I am healed of AIDS, ALS, sickle cell disease, terminal cancer, multiple sclerosis, strokes, seizures, scarlet fever, Parkinson's disease, Kawasaki disease, leukemia, blood disease, and all other disease unknown to me but known by you, I am healed.

Father, your words say whom the Son has made free they are free indeed.

I declare ~ today I'm freed forevermore, no more chains, restraints, bondage, fetters, captivities are holding me.

I will not ~ be held captive by Satan and his spiritual principalities. I bind them, and I loose life, liberty, and the pursuit of godliness in every area of life.

Chapter 27
LORD ACCORDING TO YOUR WORD

In **1 Corinthians 15:55** I decree and declare ~ I have victory over death and the grave. I superimpose the law of the Spirit of life in Christ Jesus over the law of sin and death. I decree and declare that I shall not die but live to declare your works {**Romans 8: 2, Psalms 118:17**}! In **Galatians 3:13** I believe that you Christ have redeemed me from the curse of the law.

Prayers for Emotional Healing Associated With Disease.

I command ~ anger, hostility, rage, violence, all these spirits rooted in high cholesterol, I command these spirits to come out now!

A broken spirit associated with a weak immune system come out; my immune system is strong.

All spirits of envy, jealous, and backbiting, I bind you, and I command you to come out of the bones {**James 4:5**}.

I don't want the wrath of God coming upon my life!

I bind~ and reject all spirits of pride, lust, greed which is idolatry, sexual immorality, evil desires, and I command you to come out {**James 1: 15**}!

Come out of the spine, come out of the heart, come out of the liver, come out of the spleen, come out of my sinus, come out of my kidneys, come out of my bloodline, come out of my flesh, you have no authority over me!

I rebuke ~ the spirit of Belial and decree and declare that you shall not cleave to my body {**Psalms 41:8**}. Come out, I bind you, I break you, I root you up, I destroy your works, I overthrow your power, I tear you down, I pluck you out of your dwelling place, and I command you, to loose me and let me go free {**Jeremiah 1:10**}!

I decree and declare ~ according to **Nahum 3:15** that these things shall not return a second time.

Prayer for Fire

God, you are a consuming fire. I ask the Consuming Fire to bring the enemy down before my face, drive them out and destroy them quickly.

I ask God that you make me a minister of flaming Fire, send judgment and Fire and bring your Fire upon the earth for purification, healing, and burning out disease and sicknesses.

It will cleanse, consume, protect, defend and harden me. I loose the fire of the Lord to burn up my enemies {**Nahum 3:15**}! I release the fire of the Lord to burn out everything that's not like him.

Chapter 28
CLOSING THE DOOR
TO THE ENEMY

Job 21:25, Lamentations 3: 15, Romans 3: 14, Ephesians. 4: 31 Hebrews. 12: 15, James 4: 7 Genesis 4:7, Exodus 12:22-23.

Matt 16:18: "And I say also unto thee, that thou art Peter and upon this rock I wilt build my church and the Gates of hell shall not prevail against it." Fear took hold of upon them there, and pain as of a woman in travail {**Psalms 48:6**}.

I speak peace to all anxiety that's rooted in fear. Now, in the name of Jesus, I break your power from touching my life.

I decree that I'm free of all hereditary curses of sickness and disease and command them to come out. I exercise authority over the work of God's hands.

I command ~ the devil's forces to destroy themselves. By the blood of Jesus Christ, I take dominion over Satan.

I put on the whole armor of God closing open doorways to demons and come against the kingdom of Evil. I use the word of God, Logos and Rhema against the forces of evil.

I stand ~ as with the army of the Lord's host, exercising dominion over sickness and disease. I use my tactics and weapons of war against the enemy.

I bind and loose ~ on earth what is bound and loosed in heaven. I return curses, sickness and disease and weapons forms against me.

I renounce oaths taken by my ancestors which bond their descendants. I break the curse associated with iniquities and inheritance.

I severe demonic links between my souls and spirits, and break curses from false teaching, false miracles, and words of knowledge, prophecies, and manifestation of Godliness.

I close open doorways in my body and soul as the demons leave.

I command ~ the demons to return to the sender.

I command ~ the demons of death and destruction, sickness and pain, torment and curses to go to the Abyss and the lower regions of the sea, Tartarus (where fallen angels are bound) dry places.

Chapter 29
COMMAND THE DEVIL'S FORCES TO DESTROY

Ezekiel 35:6, Jeremiah 17: 5-6, Isaiah 49: 26, 2 Corinthians. 20:23

"{When the three hundred trumpets sounded, the Lord caused the men throughout the camp to turn on each other with their swords {**Judges 7:22.**}" The army fled to Beth Shittah toward Zererah as far as the border of Abel Meholah near Tabbath". NIV

Judges 7: 22 "and the three hundred blew the trumpets and the Lord set every man sword against his fellow even throughout the host: and the host fled to Bethshittah in Zererah and the border of Abelmeholah unto Tabbath." KJV

I force ~ demons into open combat with other demons, split their army and destroy the Kingdom of Satan.

I command ~ demons to attack their own works. I command civil war in Satan's kingdom. The demons are commanded to confuse and sow terror and panic in the hearts of those practicing witchcraft and Satanism.

I cause the devil's forces to fight against each other. I return what has been sent to attack me, including the demons, principalities, powers, ruler of darkness, wickedness in high places, and command them to attack the sender.

The very trap that was set up for my demise, God causes the enemy to fall into it.

I decree and declare ~ that these things I see today, I shall not see again a second time, because you, O Lord, are bringing it to an end {**Nahum 1:9**}. Submit to God, resist the devil and he will flee {**James 4: 7**}!

Spend time in thanking, singing and praising him for the victory!

Father, I acknowledge that thine Kingdom has all the power and the glory forever. The Lord God Almighty rule, reign, and dominates. You are all-powerful; you're the all-knowing God. I melt at your feet; let your glory cover me. I thank you and praise you for healing and delivering my life from disease, sickness, infirmities, demonic spirits and the noisome pestilence. I praise you for your splendor and your holiness. Amen.

True love never grows heavy, who beloved must be love, love warms more than a thousand fires, love rules without law. Love is master of all arts. Italian Proverb - Author Unknown.

Chapter 30
HEALED BY HIS LOVE

Ephesians 3: 17-19: "That Christ may dwell in your hearts by faith that ye being rooted and ground in, may be to comprehend with all the saints what is the breadth, length, depth and height of his love, and to know the love of Christ, which passeth knowledge that ye might be filled with all the fullness of God."

His love is so amazing

"Will the Lord reject forever? Will He never show his favor again? Has his unfailing love vanished forever? Has his promised failed for all times? Has God forgotten to be merciful? Has he in anger withheld his compassion? Then I thought, "To this I will appeal the years when the Most High stretched out his right hand. I will remember the deeds of the Lord yes; I will remember your miracles of long ago. I will consider all your works and meditate on all your mighty deeds." Your ways, God are holy. What god is as great as our God? You are the God who performs miracles; you display your power among the people" **Psalms 76:7-14**

1 John 4: 18, **2 Corinthians 13:11**,

Beloved, contrary to what religion has taught, God has never stopped performing signs, wonders and miracles; he's still the greatest miracle worker ever existed. It was and still is His desire that no man should perish but live an eternal life here in the earth.

For God so loved the world that he gave his only begotten son, that whosoever believeth in him shall not perish but have eternal life" (**John 3:16**).

God has no need for any sick, diseased, or poor person in heaven. So as it is in heaven, let it also be here on earth. I decree and declare that you shall not perish/die a premature death; yet yea shall live and declare the works of the Lord (**Psalms 118:17**)

I pray now for everyone who has declared the decrees in this book will experience the power of Your love. I pray that it touch's them right now and make everything new at this moment in the name of Jesus. I use your love, God, as a weapon against the forces of evil. I give thanks to You for Your love endures forever; it never fails.

I decree and declare that everyone that prays these prayers is healed! I pray and seal these things by the power of Your blood and decree that they will not return void, but will accomplish that whereto it is sent out. Glory to a magnificent God!

Be healed for Christ sake, he has need of your body!

Eventually you will come to understand that love heals everything, and love is all there is.
- Gary

References

about.com

Amplified

Christian Apologetic Research Ministry

Dictionary.com

Savedhealed.com

King James

Ministry Magazine

New International Bible

New King James

Nuggets of Wisdom

Quotes by leaders

Strong's Concordance

Webster's Bible Dictionary

Webster's II New College Dictionary

"It came Upon a Midnight Clear" by Edmund H. Sears (1810-1876). Public domain.

"Blessed Assurance" by Fanny J. Crosby (18201915). Public domain.

(The blood) http://www.seekgod.org/message/bloodofjesus.html *Gene Moody's spiritual warfare manual.*

Cindy Trimm Rules of Engagement

Apostle Eckhardt Prayers that Rout Demons

Glossary

Abaddon

The destroyer or angel of the bottomless pit.

Abyss

Very deep, bottomless, unfathomable and boundless pit

Allow

To grant, give or yield approving, justifying or sanctioning, giving permission.

Annihilate

To destroy, vanish, cease, and be of no effect, the substance existence, to kill completely.

Authority

The power to influence, or command, the thought, opinion or behavior.

Bind

To disallow, to tie together, or confine with a cord, or anything that is flexible; to fasten as with a band, fillet or ligature.

Command

To bid; to order; to direct; to charge; implying authority and power to control and to require obedience.

Darkness

Devoid no reflection, transmission or radiation of light.

Declare

To emphatically state one's intention making known formally, officially, or explicitly.

Decree

Judicial decision or determination of a litigated cause; as a decree of the court of chancery. The decision of a court of equity is called a decree; that of a court of law, a judgment.

Disallow

To refuse to allow, denying the force, truth or validity of.

Loose

To allow, to untie or unbind; to free from any fastening, to disengage; to detach; as, to loose one's hold, To release from imprisonment; to liberate; to set at liberty

Penetrate

To pass into or through, to enter by overcoming resistance, to gain entrance.

Power

The faculty of doing or performing any thing; the faculty of moving or of producing a change in something; ability or strength.

Rebuke

To speak sharply, to turn back or keep down.

Tactics

They are or skills of employing available means to accomplish and ending goal of defeat the enemy.

Tartarus

Where fallen angels are bound
Kingdom Builders International Ministry
Tel: 595-2766 Email: kbiministries@aol.com

Printed in the United States
By Bookmasters